BEING MIKE AB

Ro

V

Paul Burton

Published in 2014 by FeedARead.com Publishing –
Arts Council funded

A CIP catalogue record for this title is available from the British Library.

Dedication

It's my honour and a great privilege to dedicate this small account of things that have passed, and hopefully will continue, to a man and his family that I came to know so many years ago and love dearly:

Sid James, Val James, Susan James and Steve James

Thank you so much for everything.

Robin Stewart

Foreword

In 1971, I was cast as Sally Abbott in *Bless this House*, and Robin was cast as my brother, Mike. Working on the series at Thames TV, set by the River Thames in Teddington, was an absolute joy. Light entertainment at that time was magical. I found myself mingling with many artistes including Tommy Cooper and Benny Hill.

Thames TV was fondly known as 'The Fun Factory'. It was a golden era of TV, which produced many great sitcoms, such as *Father, Dear Father*, *Love Thy Neighbour*, *Man About the House*, *Love Thy Neighbour*, *George and Mildred* and *Robin's Nest*.

Bless this House was a big hit in the ratings, reaching number one most weeks. This success was undoubtedly due to the brilliant Sid James, the master of comic timing. To say Sid was popular is an understatement, the public loved him and so did the cast. He was the star of the series, and he so generously created a warm, happy and a truly fun-filled atmosphere which lasted for over six years.

Diana Coupland, who played our mother, Jean Abbott, was an inspirational bit of casting by our own boss, William G. Stewart (Bill). Diana's on-screen chemistry with Sid was just delightful to watch.

Sid thought very highly of Anthony Jackson. He slipped into the role of Sid's neighbour and mate, Trevor, perfectly. Meanwhile, Patsy Rowlands, who played Trevor's wife, Betty, kept us all laughing with her natural comedy flair.

We had some lovely guest actors and actresses over the years, all of whom seemed to love working with Sid and the 'family'. Bill was very loyal to the actors he liked and admired, often casting them several times in the same roles, or even different roles, hence they became regulars.

For several years, we rehearsed each episode in a Scout hut just down the road from the studios. It was here our wonderful floor manager, the late John Lynton, would often cook us all a bacon, sausage and egg breakfast. This is just an example of the relaxed friendship that existed amongst the cast and crew.

I'm sure Robin will agree that this period of time was amongst the happiest in our careers. We had great fun and Robin always looked out for me, as any brother would for his little sister.

Sally Geeson
August 2014

Preface

It's fair to say that the actor Robin Stewart, who is best-known for having played Mike Abbott in the Thames TV sitcom, *Bless this House*, has become a bit of an enigma to his fans, both old and new, in recent times. Although they knew that this former on-screen parents in the sitcom, Sid James and Diana Coupland, had both sadly passed away, and his one-time screen sister, Sally Geeson, now made regular appearances at conventions and events, no-one seemed to know exactly what had become of Robin. The most information that comedy fans seemed able to offer was that the actor was now living and working in Australia.

Like many other people of my age group, I grew up watching repeats of *Bless this House* on TV and later bought videos and DVD of the various episodes. My career has led to me working with a number of well-known actors and actresses from the world of theatre film and TV, and I was keen to meet and work with Robin too. The internet seemed unable to offer me any confirmed information about his whereabouts, other than he was now living and working in Australia. Members of the TV industry, who had worked with Robin, confessed to knowing little more than the fans.

Then, in the early hours of one morning in 2012, I was amazed to discover a link to Robin's official website on an internet search engine. Thanks to an email address on Robins' site, I was finally able to make contact with the man himself. He revealed that he was indeed residing in Australia.

The following year, Robin revealed to me that he had moved back to the UK, but was in hospital. The opportunity to speak on the phone would, he promised, present itself once he was back home.

As good as his word, a long phone call was subsequently shared between Robin and me during the spring of 2013. This led us to discussing the idea of working on a new book together. Numerous phone calls and emails followed, as did a meeting at Elstree Studios in north London. The final result is the book you're now reading.

To summarise, *Being Mike Abbott* offers readers the opportunity to learn more about Robin's colourful life before, during and after *Bless this House*. Yes, I did say before and after, because his career has, of course, encompassed a number of other enviable roles and opportunities away from being part of the famous Abbott family.

Robin and I would like to take this opportunity to thank a number of people for their help during the process of writing this publication.

Firstly, we'd like to offer our sincere appreciation to Sid James' family for granting us permission to use the front cover photo of Sid with Robin taken from an episode of *Bless this House*.

A debt of gratitude is owed to Sally Geeson for taking the time to write the foreword, and Sid James' daughter, Susan James, for writing the afterword.

We're also extremely grateful to Candida Baker, Tony Gordon, Sue Holderness, Melinda Jackson, Françoise Pascal, Michael Pollington, Gary Shail and Gay Soper for allowing us to share their recollections within this publication.

And finally we'd like to acknowledge Jane Foster of FremantleMedia's stills department for her help with sourcing the front cover photo from archives.

Paul Burton
August 2014

Introduction

Firstly, I would like to say a big thank you for buying and reading this book. Despite not being a complete autobiography, I hope you will find these modest ramblings about my life interesting, amusing and informative.

I should make it clear that this book could never be classed as a kiss-and-tell type of a publication. So if you were hoping for any gossip of that kind, then I'm afraid that you'll be bitterly disappointed! I have also refrained from mentioning certain people who are, or were, close to me out of the deepest respect for their privacy.

There are so many people that I would like to thank here for helping to enrich my life. However, I realise that this would be terribly self-indulgent. But I would like to take this opportunity to express my sincere gratitude to my late parents, Maximilian and Dorothy, for creating me.

Being Mike Abbott may sound a strange title, given that I've been lucky enough to play a wealth of characters over the years. However, I'm more than happy to admit that I'm most remembered for playing the role of Mike Abbott.

This small publication is dedicated to the late, great Sid James. He was a true gentleman, who I was proud to have been able to call a friend. It is also dedicated to Sid's wonderful family who I am proud to say remain my friends to this day.

Robin Stewart
August 2014

Chapter One

A Sea Of Learning

'Robin, I do hope that you have said "hello" to your dressing room.'

Sir Ralph Richardson

In the first chapter, we discover how life after the Second World War led Robin's parents to settling in London with their son after their travels. We also discover how, despite an inauspicious start to his life, a chance meeting with a Disney talent scout, was to subsequently propel Robin into the acting profession. This leads to reminiscences of appearing in the West End with Sir Ralph Richardson and Phyllis Calvert, sharing the Broadway stage with Richard Burton, and the small screen with Ingrid Bergman.

Life before *Bless this House* was a sea of learning, scholastically minimal, yet, in real life terms, a collection of experiences that, had I missed them, would have been a crime. The good, the bad, the hurtful and the extremely amusing – all of which have created the person I am today.

Before settling in England, my mother, Dorothy Evelyn Steuer, nee Beer, who played and taught the piano, travelled extensively from India to Brazil before returning to India. It was the advent of the Second World War that led her to joining the WAF (Women's Air Force) and to living in India. During her posting to India, my mother met Maximilian Steuer, later to become my father, who had recently joined his brother, Hugo Steuer, in working in his pharmaceutical business. As well as spending time in India, my mother and father also spent time in Tibet.

When my father's older brothers and his sister left home to take up other professions, he decided that it was his duty to become the black sheep of the family and spent all his time playing chess, poker, bridge and backgammon. In his defence, he did at one time try his hand at being a tailor and cutter in London. But after just three weeks of being gainfully employed, he lost interest. Instead, he spent most of his time playing chess or in casinos playing his favourite card games in cafes.

My mother's promising career as a concert pianist ended due to the war. Although she did continue to give piano lessons until she became disillusioned with teaching children who had been forced into tinkling the ivories by their parents.

My mother later become great friends with the violinist, Yehudi Menuhin, and one his two sisters, Hephzibah Menuhin. Later, when they were all living in London, all three would make visits to the famous Abbey Road Studios to play together. This was simply for their own amusement, and was long before The Beatles started to record there!

I was born in Reardon Nursing Home in Wood Street, Calcutta, on 9 October 1946. My mother had typhoid and I weighed in at just 2lb. It wasn't an auspicious start and I wasn't expected to live, but Robin Guy Henry Steuer – my real name – obviously had other ideas! At the time, India was still a British colony, so I was issued with a birth certificate showing me to be British, even though my father was stateless.

After the war things were still a struggle for my parents. Jews were still stateless and a Czech couldn't go back home, even if they wanted to, as it was occupied by Russia. We eventually moved to London, where my father continued to play and gamble on chess, poker, bridge and backgammon. Meanwhile, my mother worked in the buying department of John Lewis in Oxford Street.

My father was always a bit of an enigma. For example, I once complained about a pain in my right foot. It was because I had a bruised arch as I had inherited my mother's slim feet with a high arch, it was quite painful. My father, Maximilian, listened to my tale of woe with a totally expressionless face and then walked over to me and ground his heal into my left foot. I was not very happy and vocalised my disapproval.

'What on earth are you complaining about now?' he said. 'They must surely both feel the same, so there's no difference or comparison in the pain factor. So get on with the day.'

On another memorable occasion I sat down to breakfast and was presented with a bowl of porridge. I was not overly impressed, and didn't eat it. At lunchtime I was surprised when the porridge was once again put in front of me. Needless to say, I did not touch it. It was there again at dinner and once again I declined to eat it. When at breakfast the next day the same bowl was given to me again, I looked up at my father for some kind of explanation.

'Well, it doesn't look too good does it?' he remarked. 'That skin isn't very appealing and it looks quite solid. I should eat it now as it will only get worse.'

It soon became obvious to me that I wasn't going to win this battle with my father. So, with as little gagging as possible, I ate the hard and horrible solution!

Some people said my father was a hard man, but he just had a unique way of getting his message across. I don't think I suffered from his approach to getting me to face the ups and downs of the world. But I personally have tried to be just a little more tolerant and kinder in my attitude to others. Although I must admit that the older I get the less I am finding it tolerable to accept other peoples ways of justifying there reasons for being right. A little more humility, and a less pedantic attitude, will always get a better result from someone educated by Maximilian.

My father's chess and poker cronies always told me he was very proud of me, but I don't ever remember him ever saying it to me personally. I have always tried to make others feel important. I have been so lucky with the people that I have worked with over the years. On the whole, I can safely say that I have worked with some of the most professional people you could ever hope to meet.

Memories of my father are varied, but they mainly involve the chess board. He believed that chess was ultimately the perfect murder as your adversary would seldom see their fate until it was far too late. Dad was basically a gambler with his chess and bridge. There were times that he played backgammon for high stakes, but it was mainly chess and bridge that kept his brain working. He always had to be in control of the odds, and his game plan did not seem to recognise losing!

My earliest recollections of my father are of monks and solitude. He was fascinated by the Buddhist way of life. Although my father was brought up in a Jewish household, as far as a race was concerned, the only time that my father went to a Synagogue was to pray for the dead, and to pay his respects to his parents who unfortunately did not survive the Holocaust. They sadly ended their lives in the concentration camp gas chambers. Both my father and his elder brother were

Buddhists. His brother was also a Mason and created a lodge in India in the late Thirties. The time we spent together in monasteries in Tibet were quite amazing experiences. The tranquillity and the peace that surrounded us within their walled seclusion has stayed with me to this day.

I remember Dad being nick-named a married bachelor. And although I truly believe that he loved my mother with a passion, he desperately needed his freedom. His days would start around midday and just continue until he finished whatever he was doing. This could take days and days – and nights and nights! I never knew where he was or what he was up to!

As I think back to my early childhood years, the memories of my life in London come flooding back. There were my many visits to Kenwood House in Hampstead, and the coaching houses of yesteryear, where one could enjoy afternoon tea overlooking another stunning lake and more woodland scenery. Then walking on to Hampstead Heath's famous Whitestone Pond, where sailboat and power driven speed boats entertained the onlookers who stopped to marvel at the boat enthusiasts at play.

Hampstead Heath used to play host to the 'donkey man'. He used to religiously trundle his donkeys from Swiss Cottage all the way up to Fitzjohns Avenue and then onto the back road to Whitestone Pond to give rides to the waiting children. It was rumoured that one Sunday his father was sitting in his cart while going back down the hill to Swiss Cottage when his lead donkey suddenly took great offence. The donkey is said to have kicked the cart, and its occupant, to shredded bits of timber, therefore causing his demise. I never did pluck up the courage to ask the 'donkey man' if this story was true or not. But it could go a long way to explaining why the 'donkey man' was prone to being very bad-tempered.

Occasionally my friends and I would walk a donkey up the hill for the 'donkey man', round and round the track, then ride one home. For this, we got strong legs and five bob for our efforts. This was a reality check, as I was working with the cows at the Express Dairy model farm in Temple Fortune!

The route I often used to take from from Hampstead Health then continued to meander, as it still does to this day, down to Primrose Hill. From there, I could go over the Regent's Park Canal and into Regent's Park, which joins north London to Baker Street.

In the middle of Regent's Park is the inner circle, and the most beautiful array of gardens, which houses Regent's Park Open Air Theatre. I can still visualise all the green strips that had acorns which made interesting armies when used matchsticks or tooth picks were thrust into them, making them resemble a fighting collection of foot soldiers. This was ideal for those of us who couldn't afford the delights of Hamleys or Gamages where expensive lead replicas could be purchased. They could then be painted to resemble any army you desired. With the advent of my first theatrical job, buying toy soldiers, and other such novel items, suddenly became accessible to me overnight.

Regent's Park was an ideal place for me to go to collect conkers. Once a piece of string was added to a conker, they become objects for competitive groups of boys to do battle with in bitter playground competitions. Boys would often claim to owning a champion nut that had fought many a battle. But after being bashed to bits by a victorious younger, a harder conker soon went on to become the talk of the playground!

One afternoon, while I was walking along Avenue Road, which runs between Swiss Cottage and Regent's Park, a car stopped. The driver wound down his window and thrust a business card into my hand. Thinking nothing of it, I put the card in my pocket and watched the man as he drove away. I shrugged and carried on with my quest to find acorns. My mother was not in the slightest bit impressed when I gave her the card upon returning home. However, after I was given a rude awakening on both cheeks of my posterior, she called the number. The driver turned out to be a Disney scout. Through him I duly met Flavia Pickworth, who, in turn, put me in touch with Progressive Management, which was run by Neil Landor. Landor was an ex-BBC radio presenter who played an incredibly important part in my formative years as an actor. I say actor, because at the time I was but an eleven year-old boy who, ironically, at the time had no real desire to perform.

In 1959, I auditioned to play Sir Ralph Richardson and Phyllis Calvert's son, Robin Rhodes, in Graham Greene's *The Complaisant Lover*. The two-act comedy is set in the home of Rhodes' family and in a guesthouse in Amsterdam. The play itself revolves around an affair that takes place between Mary Rhodes and Clive Root, who's a friend of her husband, Victor Rhodes.

My audition for the production, which was directed by John Gielgud, was deemed successful and I duly became one of two boys who shared the role. We had to share the role due to the strict law governing childhood actors. We also understudied each other.

The cast for the play, which was staged at the Globe Theatre (renamed the Gielgud Theatre in 1995) on Shaftesbury Avenue in London, also included Paul Scofield, Julia Lockwood and Gerald Flood. A quick check of archive records reminded me that the play's press night took place on 18 June 1959.

Watching Sir Ralph create magic on that celebrated stage night after night was something I have never forgotten. His mastery of the dribbling glass, and the silent tears at the realisation that his beloved wife was having an affair, created the loudest silence I have ever experienced in a theatre, bar none.

I shall also never forget the day Sir Ralph took me aside and spoke to me.

'Robin, I do hope that you have said "hello" to your dressing room,' he said.

I must have looked somewhat bemused, because he then proceeded to explain himself. He reasoned that as the room afforded me the luxury of being able to leave the persona of Robin Stewart there while I was onstage, it was important that I said 'hello' to the room and thanked it for its kindness. To this day, much to people's annoyance, I continue talk to rooms, as well as trees and animals!

My wage at the time was fifteen pounds a week. This was a veritable fortune for a twelve year-old – especially as the average wage was around seven to ten pounds a week at the time! I felt very wealthy as I donned my new overcoat and trudged my way through the snow to the theatre during the winter.

Leaving the stage door at the back of the Globe Theatre reveals an alley way that leads you out to the hustle and bustle of Shaftesbury Avenue, complete with its theatres and bright lights. Getting there was another matter, though, as I used to have to negotiate the stage door stalwarts who, without fail, would tell you whether they'd heard you from the 'gods' or not. The 'gods' is a theatrical term, which refers to the highest parts of a theatre, such as the upper balconies, which is invariably where these avid theatre-goers sat. They all believed they knew exactly who was destined for greatness in the profession. Their opinion was formed purely on whether a particular actor could be heard from the two bob seats or not. These theatrical purists were always very polite and full of advice. They were totally dedicated to the cause, queued for hours and sat on little three-seater canvas chairs. Even now, all these years later, I can still visualise them now chatting amongst themselves and recalling who they had imparted their wisdom to just the previous night. I loved them all, and they were always kind to me.

Next in line for me was a small role in an ATV drama called *Deadline Midnight*. The series was set in a fictitious Fleet Street newspaper called *The Daily Globe.* It was taped at ATV's then Borehamwood-base during 1960 and 1961. Armine Sandford, Glyn Houston, Jeremy Young and Peter Vaughan all had appeared at one time or another during the run. I personally was cast as a Polish refugee who believed his father (played by George Pravada) was a hero.

Although ATV, who were once an ITV-franchise-holder, no longer exists, the former film studio where *Deadline Midnight* was made is now home to the long-running BBC continuing dramas, *EastEnders* and *Holby City*.

Fate was to again take a guiding hand in my acting career when I found himself being cast in the Walt Disney film, *Greyfriars Bobby*. I can't remember exactly when I filmed my scenes, however, the film was originally released in 1961.

The story of the film, which is set in Scotland in 1865, focusses on a Skye terrier, called Bobby, who refuses to be parted from his owner, Auld Jock, after he dies of pneumonia. The heartbroken dog takes to sleeping next to his late owner's grave in the Greyfriars' kirkyard, and refuses to be adopted. The caretaker of the graveyard, James Brown (Donald Crisp), tries to discourage Bobby from holding vigil at the graveside. But this does nothing to deter the dog who, as time goes on, finds himself melting the hearts of the local residents, not least the children. Eventually, Bobby, now a Freeman of the City of Edinburgh, is adopted by the community, and he's saved from the risk of being destroyed.

The heart-warming production boasted, amongst other others, Donald Crisp, Laurence Naismith, Alex Mackenzie, Kay Walsh, Andrew Cruickshank and Gordon Jackson in the cast. The latter-named actor, of course, went on to find TV fame playing Hudson in *Upstairs Downstairs*, and as George Cowley in *The Professionals*. I played the small role of the Lord Provost's secretary, Jodie Ross, complete with a Scottish accent.

In addition to being filmed on location in Scotland, the movie was made at Shepperton Studios in Middlesex. The set, complete with cobble stone roads and houses galore, was built in the largest sound stage Shepperton had at that time.

I will never forget the charming way that the little dog, who played Bobby, was trained. It was an education all on its own! He had a squeaky toy and all you had to do was hold it in your hand and squeeze and he would follow you anywhere. Not surprisingly, everybody loved him!

Not so memorable, was that those of us of school age had to take lessons at the studio. These were taken by a man wearing a double-breasted jacket who always sounded like he had a plum in his mouth whenever he spoke. Of course, that was how everybody sounded in the film industry at the time – whether they were in-front or behind the camera!

As well as representing yours truly, Neil Landour looked after several other actors, including a young Jane Asher, and made a pretty good living. Being of old BBC stock, I don't think I ever saw him dressed in anything other than a three-piece suit, or carvery twills, and a blue double-breasted jacket. He was a very dapper individual who was a sort of god in our eyes.

In 1960, Jane Asher and I appeared in a stage play together called *Will You Walk a Little Faster*. Michael Glynn and Diana Churchill played our parents. We toured the usual theatres in the provinces before moving to the Duke of York's Theatre in London's West End. The pre-London tour included Blackpool, Southampton and Brighton. We stayed in boarding houses around the country and were served a number of heavenly fried breakfasts each morning. The only real disappointment was having to obey a chaperone at all times. There was no misbehaving of any sorts back in those days!

Sadly, *Will You Walk a Little Faster* finished under a wee cloud. Business was bad at the box office, and the size of the audiences was simply not big enough to sustain the costs of staging a play in the West End. It's an age old problem that continues to haunt many a theatre producer.

While I was still appearing at the Duke of York's, my agent, Neil, took me to another theatre in London, where there was a line of boys queuing outside. Neil simply ignored the line and walked straight up to the stage door. He walked up to an important looking lady waiting there that we were going down onto the stage – and that's what we did! I still had no idea of what I was there for as we stood at the front of the stage. Presently, Neil spoke to someone in the auditorium.

‘When do you want Robin to leave for Canada?’ he asked.

‘It’ll have to be a week on Wednesday when he turns fourteen,’ someone replied from the dark.

I realise now that I probably made a million enemies in one foul swoop!

Little did I realise that I would be spending my fourteenth birthday in 1960 meeting the actor Richard Burton on stage at the O’Keefe Centre in Toronto, Canada. This was the first port of call for a pre-Broadway tour of the musical version of *Camelot*.

My mother came with me as my chaperone. I am eternally grateful that she did as between my sixteenth and seventeenth birthday my dear, dear mother, friend and soul mate passed away. Her will to live was never in question, but I think that between my father’s lifestyle, and my early independence, we simply wore her out. Her main solace in life was the Friends Meeting House in Hampstead, as she was a devout Quaker. When she played the piano it was like an air of magic filling the room. Every animal in the house used to come and sprawl out around her. Mum introduced me to elephants, wolves, literature and, of course, the piano. For my sins I have not touched the piano since she died. She was always there when I needed her the most. Our long walks on Hampstead Heath always ending up at Kenwood House where we would talk about all aspects of life over a tea and a bun. She was truly special human being who put others before herself. She was taken from us far too soon, and I still miss her greatly.

I had to rehearse my role for *Camelot* on the plane flying to Canada. My excitement was curtailed briefly when I was whisked away to the hotel on our arrival in Toronto so I could get some sleep. Later, after I was fully rested, I was spirited away to the theatre and introduced to my dresser.

Back in England I always had to climb up lots of stairs to a dressing room in the highest part of the theatre, but not at the O'Keefe! No, at the O'Keefe I was able to use a lift with piped music. More importantly, I had a tannoy system in my dressing room which meant I could hear where we were in the show.

When the last scene was being set, which was the fall of Camelot, Richard Burton, as King Arthur, stood alone on the stage. There was a lonely tent positioned near to the legendary actor, behind which a small boy – me – stood nervously with his dresser, patiently waiting for his cue. This would be the very first time I had met Burton – on stage and in front of thousands of people. All of whom, of course, had no idea that I had just flown in from England.

My big moment finally came and my newly-met dresser stamped his foot, smiled, raised a thumb in an off-you-go sort of gesture, and, with a gentle push, there I was walking towards King Arthur on a lonely stage in Toronto. Franz Allers, our famed conductor, raised his baton and the orchestra gently swelled. Richard asked me who was hiding behind the tent. I made my entrance and a whole new chapter in my life began.

In no time at all both of us, in character, were looking up at the upper circle. One had just lost Camelot and his Queen, and the other, a small page called Tom Mallory, was drawing tears from the audience. All was going well. Sadly, however, this is where we discovered for the very first time that I couldn't sing! We were both supposed to sing the signature song 'Camelot' together. The words 'A law was passed a distant while ago here,' had never sounded quite like this before! No-one knew the panic. No-one had the slightest idea that it wasn't how it was supposed to sound. The audience was totally wrapped up in the King and the small boy trying to resurrect a broken dream. Sir Pellinore appeared as if by magic, and King Arthur requested that I kneel before him. Then the trusty sword came falling down onto my shoulders and my character was knighted in front of over two thousand people. The music swelled once more and our voices melted together as the curtain came down to 'Camelot' sung by the King and a newly-knighted young lad. There were several curtain calls and much cheering and standing of an audience caught up in the fantasy that was *Camelot*.

The reviews were out by midnight, but were not the best. Everyone was waiting for them. It was a bigger buzz than the West End of London. It seemed as if the whole world revolved around what the press thought. It was all so alien to this fourteen year-old boy who had only just stepped off the plane and into a world that he had never ever dreamed was possible. The critics said that the production was too long. They also said felt the composers Lerner and Loewe were basically just trading on their previous successes.

The rehearsal call set for the next morning was the start of the trimming process the likes of which I had never seen before – or since! Of course, way down on the list was the fact that Sir Tom could not sing and the chorus now had the job of swelling the last scene from the wings! Oh the shame indeed! And that was my first night on stage in what was to become a sure fired hit on Broadway for many years to come.

The production then travelled from Toronto to Boston. The route taken by most of the plays heading for Broadway was either Boston or Philadelphia. We played for five weeks in Boston, and I must have talked to every squirrel that lived in the park in the middle of town! I also took part in radio interviews that were beamed out right across America – not something a little kid would be allowed to do now!

Richard and I went riding in the Blue Hills outside Boston, with an old campaigner called Al. He was in his late sixties and had over a hundred horses that roamed the hills. He also knew the fastest tracks through the woods to the pancake outlet that was strategically placed on a highway that traversed its way through the mountains. What a treat that was! He knew everything that there was to know about horses and their little foibles. Here was a man made of sinew and muscle and had a smile that shone like the sun coming up over the hills.

It was written into our contracts that we were not allowed to do sports that were considered in any way dangerous. For some unknown reason the riding of strangely coloured equines in the Blue Hills was not on Richards' list of dangerous things to do. Then again, for a man from a Welsh mining town, a slightly overgrown pit pony is not considered exactly dangerous!

In Boston, I experienced the peace and tranquillity of another Friends Meeting House. My Mum, being a devout Quaker, was overjoyed to find solace in the slightly larger than life city of. Coming from England and its comparative gentility, Boston was quite a shock, even in those days!

After five weeks in the plush hotel in Boston, we left for New York, and the beginning of the Broadway run at the Majestic Theater. What an experience that was!

We lived on West 72nd and Park Avenue right on Central Park. There was a television in each room and for me that was just the bee's knees as my father wouldn't allow a TV in our home back in London. We had a radio, and that was it. But here there were more channels than I had ever dreamed of. There was also pizza at fifteen cents a slice. The tomato and cheese-based flat pieces of pizza dough that you could watch being twirled from outside the window was an adventure all on its own. So this was New York in all its glory!

It was during this period that I attended PCS. That was the Professional Children's School in New York. While I was there, my agent in New York got me the part of Ingrid Bergman's son in the CBS production of *Twenty-Four Hours in a Woman's Life*.

During the filming we shot a scene where I had to stand next to Ingrid in a grave yard. Holding her hand was like being connected to a furnace at full heat. It felt like her whole feelings and heart just came through her body and into my hand. She was a powerhouse without being a violent fire, yet the heat that came from just her very presence was unbelievable. The flame that rose inside her was like a living being. Not a word was spoken, but the power was so strong that you could have roasted an elephant on its embers, let alone the sheer power that the heat created.

The journey back to the theatre on Broadway each night after the filming was quite unique. We used to race through the crowded streets in an ambulance with the siren blaring at full volume. I never did establish if it was a real ambulance or a pretend one owned by the studio. The main thing was that I had to be back to the theatre by the end of the interval. Fortunately, I only ever missed one performance.

I remember that two dancers in *Camelot* – Dick Kutch and Dick Gains – took my mother and me to a Chinese restaurant in China Town. One of the best restaurants in town was situated next door. It was so expensive, that the average person simply couldn't afford to eat there.

My other memories of New York included eating at Downey's Steak House, which had photographs of famous actors who had visited over the years on the wall. I also recall opening a cab door only to have someone jump into it and have the car drive off without me! They used to say that the best way to have a nervous breakdown was to drive a cab in New York. I don't know how true that was, but I figure that it was pretty close to the mark!

The strange thing is that I can't ever remember being scared of being in New York. Yes, it was big and possibly a little daunting, however, I was never worried by it all. There must have been threats all around me, but if there were, then I was just never conscious of them. All too quickly it became the norm. It's really strange how as a young person one gets used to ones surroundings so quickly.

When I think back to those *Camelot* days in 1960, I realise how incredible it all was. Julie Andrews, who was also in the cast, was only a young women but already a West End and Broadway star. Julie held audiences in a trance as she sang like an angel on the stage of the Majestic Theatre. Every eye watched her virginal, yet flirtatious, performance as Guinevere, a character set to become Arthur's Queen.

One night I recall Julie came off stage looking rather upset.

'It's like working with children out there sometimes,' she said with a huge sigh.

Julie was, and remains, an amazing perfectionist. You could set your watch by her moves on stage as they were so precise and exact. On the other side of the coin, meanwhile, was Richard Burton, a man whose pure energy and persona enraptured your very soul and spirit, and was the sensual magnate and the pride of his contemporaries. He dominated the stage with his presence in a way that not only carried the other actors, but carried the audience into his world. His first wife, Sybil, would eventually open a nightclub in New York, while Richard opened the start of his romantic and often volatile relationship with Elisabeth Taylor.

Life was to later offer me the unforgettable opportunity to stay with Richard Burton and Elizabeth Taylor in Rome when they were filming at Dino De Laurentiis Studios. During this visit I can I remember sitting in the Via Veneto having late night coffee before strolling to the nearby Dave's Bar. Dave (no-one seemed to know his second name!) was an amazing character from England who had set himself up as a sort of icon to the stars in Rome. It's fair to say that anybody who was out there and in the film industry in those days used to frequent Dave's Bar. I can even remember seeing Clint Eastwood propping up the bar. Not surprisingly, the place never stopped buzzing with banter and laughter!

At about three thirty in the morning of I would go to the Seta Bella. That was where all the night clubbers ended up to eat hot doughnuts and drink iced coffee. We probably all looked ridiculous dressed in our late Sixties attire, despite thinking we were all very with it. Although, to be fair, by that time of the morning most of us were very much without it – whatever it might have been at the time! We were the pretty people of that era and nothing was of greater importance except that it would all happen again tomorrow after a day of sleeping by the pool.

Meanwhile, back in New York, my last night was unbelievable. Mum and I sat in a box in the auditorium watching the show while another little boy, this time an American, was playing my much treasured part of Sir Tom. At the curtain call I had tears in my eyes as the large cast turned to us and bowed a fond farewell. Then we suddenly found ourselves back in England, and my Broadway experience suddenly felt like a long lost dream.

Chapter Two

Finding Myself

'Robin, my dear boy, do you have any idea how one may stop this grand creature, if and when the opportunity ever arises?'

Sir Alec Guinness

In this chapter we discover how Robin's fledgling acting career was to see him travel to Spain to appear in the film, H.M.S. Defiant, *join the cast of a science fiction film series,* Masters of Venus, *and tread the boards again in the West End show,* Billy Bunter Meets Magic. *Robin also explains how he briefly took time out of his career to 'find himself' during a memorable trip to East Africa, and later ended up sharing a conspiratorial chat on the set of* Cromwell, *with the legendary Sir Alec Guinness.*

With a screenplay by Nigel Kneale and Edmund H. North, *HMS Defiant* (also released as *Damn the Defiant!)* was an adaptation of a novel by Frank Tilsley. Set around time of the 'Spithead Mutiny', the film gives a dramatised, yet surprisingly realistic, view of the sea-faring goings on faced by the crews who were part of the British navy during the era. Navy press gangs, bad living conditions, extreme corporal punishment and mutiny are all part of the film's plot.

Sir Alec Guinness starred as Captain Crawford, a man whose takes command of a fictitious British warship, H.M.S. Defiant, at the start of the Napoleonic Wars in 1787. Crawford is in constantly engaged in mental warfare with his second-in-command, Lieutenant Scott-Padget (Dirk Bogarde). It's the latter whose penchant for inflicting corporal punishment on the crew is given full reign when the captain take ill.

A host of stars and up and coming actors lent their talent to this well-acted voyage. As well as Guinness and Bogarde, Robin, as Midshipman Pardoe, shared the film with the likes of Anthony Quayle, Maurice Denham, Ray Brooks, Tom Bell, and one-half of *The Likely Lads*, James Bolam. The production was directed by Lewis Gilbert, who went on to direct *Alfie*, *Educating Rita* and three James Bond films.

I still had to have a chaperone at the time, and mine was David Robinson's mother. David played Midshipman Harvey Crawford in the film. His Mum used to get very seasick when we used to travel out to the ship for filming each day on a barge.

Because of the large number of cast, extras and crew that used to be on-board during the filming, the ship used to get really hot. Once, in order to get some fresh air and to cool down, I thought it would be a good idea to climb up to the crow's nest. It was quite a complicated and daring climb to get up to there, but I somehow managed it. Eventually, while I was taking forty winks, panic set in as no-one could find me. As you can imagine, this didn't make me very popular!

We sailed in fishing boats from both Denia and Gandia to the main vessels we used during the filming. The quays at both of the ports, as with many of the ports in those days across the continent, had their main sewerage outlets slap bang in the middle of the foreshore. It was right there that the best little fishes could be caught. Apparently, the effluent carried with it a variety of succulent morsels if you were a fish. Small squids would also linger around the outlet into the ocean. It was not long before the local Spanish fisherman found a new and very amusing game to add to their days. The idea was to throw a small, but yet quite frightening squid, caught near the outlet, onto unsuspecting passing thespians – including myself. I well remember the unpleasant feeling of a squid clinging onto my chest for dear life with its many suckers. Seeing a fully grown man waving their arms about and screeching like a fisher woman must have been quite a sight for the locals!

Boredom on the vessel at sea was in abundance during the filming. Thankfully, complimentary Coca Cola and other drinks, including Spanish beer housed in large cane baskets, was a morale booster for the underpaid Spanish extras. They also entertained themselves with various practical jokes. One involved putting very small pebbles down the rifle musket barrels being used on the film. This sent the pebbles hurtling into the back or chest of anyone nearby when they let off the blank cartridges. The pain we experienced from this 'joke' was far worse than the pain inflicted by your typical angry squid!

Another favourite pastime of the extras involved hanging festering bits of pork on long lines that would suddenly appear in front of a seasick actor who was leaning over the side of the ship. The sight of this unappetising food had the immediate desired effect of making the thespian sick.

I must admit that the film kept me employed for a long time on location in Spain and then back in England. However, in our business, working on a film for a long time does not guarantee that all your scenes won't end up on the cutting room floor! I remember when Richard O'Sullivan worked on *Cleopatra* in Rome. Richard was there for about seven or eight months, and probably went to the studio for maybe no-more than week in total. He ended up spending more time travelling backwards and forwards to England each weekend to support Chelsea, and playing charity football matches, then being in front of the camera!

There were many mishaps on *Defiant*. For instance, a thin yet unfortunately wielded rapier type blade entered one actor's side and then reappeared from his back. Thankfully, apart from a stay in hospital and a lasting scar, there was no major damage done.

I remember the fight arranger, William Hobbs, battling the effects of the salt that the spray from the waves sent across the ships bows as it rested behind his contact lenses. It turned his eyes into red puddles of screaming anguish. I came across William again when I was visiting the actor Robin Nedwell at Central School of Speech and Drama in Swiss Cottage. He had become their fencing master or coach in an attempt to avoid eye-watering film locations!

Mentioning Robin Nedwell, who became famous for appearing in the LWT sitcom, *Doctor in the House*, reminds me of a story. Robin won everyone's hearts when he was at drama school. He was once asked to portray an animal of some description during a drama performance that I attended. He left the obvious lions and tigers and flamboyant flamingos to his fellow students, and decided upon playing a tortoise instead. This was a brilliant choice as he could basically spend an hour sleeping in any position he felt like. When a very puzzled drama teacher bravely walked over to him and asked what he was doing, Nedwell was ready with a clever response.

'Being a tortoise is a very slow and thought provoking process,' he said. 'Forgive me for saying so, but you're ruining it.'

He then proceeded to pretend to become a tortoise again, while giving a knowing wink to the audience.

We all knew from that moment on that Robin would become a comedy performer. I really miss him.

Sorry, I got side-tracked, let's get back to *H.M.S. Defiant*. A funny incident that has stayed with me concerns one of the stunt men. He swam with great speed towards a rescue boat during the filming of a particular scene. This followed a long and incredibly dangerous decent into the sea from the rigging of the ship. He could clearly be heard screaming: 'shark' – even though there wasn't one! All the unit laughed loudly at his exaggerated freestyle as he tried at great haste not to be eaten by the imaginary water creature.

Some of the other stories I could mention involved the antics that took place on the beach at night! Being that it was the Sixties, and Spain was a staunch Catholic country, the local police had a great time arresting crew members for indulgencing in horizontal refreshment under the moonlight! Sadly, being that I was still of chaperone age, I was never allowed to go to the beach to join in the fun and frolics with my older colleagues.

I believe that the next acting job I did was *Masters of Venus*, with Amanda Coxell and Ferdy Mayne.

Produced by A. Frank Bundy and directed by Ernest Morris, *Masters of Venus* was an eight-part science fiction film series made by Wallace Productions and the Children's Film Foundation. It was first released in UK cinemas in September 1962. Michael Barnes wrote each of the screenplays based on a story by H. B. Gregory.

The storyline features two siblings – Pat and Jim Ballantyne – who find accidentally themselves being blasted into space and bound for Venus on their father's space ship, Astarte. This unscheduled launch is courtesy of Venusian saboteurs. But fear not, the world ends up being saved when the children, and a set of grown up astronauts, prevent an interplanetary war.

Here's a list of the eight episode titles:

List Of Episodes

Episode One	Sabotage
Episode Two	Lost in Space
Episode Three	The Men With Six Fingers
Episode Four	The Thing In The Crater
Episode Five	Prisoners Of Venus
Episode Six	The Killer Virus
Episode Seven	Kill On Sight
Episode Eight	Attack

Thinking about this series reminds me that my agent, for the sum of ten shillings, used to spend an hour each week making sure that my diction was spot on. I came across a clip on YouTube recently in which I sounded as if I had just left Stowe or Wellington. I was delivering lines such as: 'Petaaaa Petaaaaaa, have you got your oxygennnn?' and 'Petaaaaa Petaaaa, please answer, there's a good chap'.

When I was about sixteen years-old, I was suddenly summoned into my agent's office. Neil had apparently spotted me from his taxi in Trafalgar Square wearing a green corduroy jacket with a 'Ban the Bomb' sign pinned to the lapel. He mentioned that he'd also seen me speaking to a small group of people who he believed were Beatniks. He felt strongly that someone who was signed to his agency should not be seen conversing with such people in public. I could see no reason for my self-opinionated agent to come to this conclusion. We parted company as agent and client and within two weeks I was left feeling confused and worthless. Neil had been my first real guide and protector in this business, so I felt lost without him.

I then went on to appear in *Tamahine*, a British comedy film made by ABPC (Associated British Picture Corporation). Directed by Philip Leacock, *Tamahine* saw Nancy Kwan playing a Polynesian woman who leaves her South Pacific island home to live with Charles Poole (Dennis Price). Poole is her father's cousin, and the headmaster of Hallow, a fictitious all-male English school. Tamahine's womanly charms don't go unnoticed by Charles' son, Richard Poole (John Fraser), and the school's art master, Clove (Derek Nimmo), and before long both men fall in love with her. And while Charles and Clove wrestle with their feelings for the new visitor, Charles starts to question the validity of his life and career.

Other well-known faces in the cast included Coral Browne, Dick Bentley, Michael Gough and Allan Cuthbertson.

As well as being filmed at Elstree Studios in Borehamwood, Hertfordshire, the film was shot on location in in beautiful Tahiti, and at Wellington College, a real boys' boarding school in Crowthorne, Berkshire. At one stage, we all stayed at Skindles Hotel in Maidenhead on the River Thames. Sadly, I never got to go on location to Tahiti – shame!

I was sad to discover that Skindles Hotel has apparently become neglected of late. It was built in 1743 and was formerly a coaching inn called the Orkney Arms. Later, in 1833, William Skindle turned into a hotel. Well known guests who stayed there during its heyday included Winston Churchill and Princess Margaret.

I remember the actress Justine Lord, who played Diana in the film, coming down to breakfast one morning desperate to part with some gossip. She announced quite casually at the breakfast table that she'd heard that a guy had been arrested for doing 'strange things' to a cow in a paddock. Apparently he did this while standing in an elevated position on an orange box. The mind boggles!

We were given permission to use the snooker room at Wellington College. Between matches, we'd listen to stories of how the boys played rugby with Stow. It was filmed in the school breaks so we could have the run of the building without getting the way of school life.

One of my biggest delights over the years has been watching all those people that I respect as actors achieving professional success. For instance, I first met Derek Fowlds when we did *Tamahine*, and a more fun loving and out there person you could not hope to meet. His appearances in programmes such as *Yes, Minister* and *Heartbeat* have given so many people a great deal of pleasure over the years. Oh yes, and we mustn't forget that Derek once accompanied Basil Brush on some of his early TV shows!

I will never forget a pantomime that I appeared in at the Shaftsbury Theatre in the West End. The production was called *Billy Bunter Meets Magic*. It started on Monday 23 December 1963 and ran daily at 2.30pm until 18 January 1964. Meanwhile, the musical *How to Succeed in Business Without Really Trying* continued to play at the same theatre in the evenings, with late afternoon matinees on Friday and Saturdays.

The magical aspect of the production was courtesy of David Nixon, who was a big star at that time. Thanks to the internet, I recently came across an article in an edition of a publication called *Collectors' Digest*, dated October 1963, and priced two shillings, which previewed the show and Nixon's involvement. It brought back many memories.

Here's an extract from the article:

DAVID NIXON GOES TO GREYFRIARS

David Nixon, one of the most-likeable personalities on television, joins the cast of the Bunter show in the West End this coming Christmas season. With the intriguing title of *Billy Bunter Meets Magic*, the play, which opens at the Shaftesbury Theatre on December 23rd, would seemed assured of success.

David Nixon plays a conjuror who can do wonderful tricks when he is all alone, but finds things go wrong when anyone else is present. And when Billy Bunter happens to be present – well, imagination boggles. In recent years there have been a few minor grumbles because the Greyfriars chums have spent Christmas abroad. This year they are in good old England – at a lonely place in Cornwall – and surely many hearts will warm spontaneously when we say the place has been named Polpelly.

Peter Bridgemont, who was an outstanding success last year, once again plays Billy Bunter. When he meets David Nixon, who plays a conjuror who has a mild flair for villainy, things really happen.

Last year the Billy Bunter show, though it did the best business of all the Christmas matinee shows, was hard hit by the weather. Another bad season would mean the end of the stage attraction. Let us hope for good weather, and give the show every support in our power. If you can display a bill profitably, let us know here at the Digest Office, and we will send one to you.

Make an early appointment to see Billy Bunter and the Greyfriars chums, not forgetting Mr. Quelch, when *Billy Bunter Meets Magic* at the Shaftesbury Theatre. More news in editions of the *Collectors' Digest.*

A number of terrible things were done to Nixon's doves during the run, which had to appear at each performance from behind a small curtain. Quite often their colours had to change from white to pink. Such things would never be allowed now!

I played Harry Wharton, the leader of the Famous Five, with characters like Inky and all of the other Enid Blyton crew. Two of the schoolboys were played by young actors who had both appeared in a stage version the previous Christmas. No less than fifty boys auditioned, including me, of course, for the remaining three schoolboy roles.

On one occasion I can remember I was banging on the wall of the set saying lines like: 'I know there's a secret opening here somewhere,' expecting at any moment the hidden door would open and our escape route shown to all the children in the audience. After a lot of banging and imploring the door to appear, I looked over at the prompt corner only to see the stage manager and other members of the stage crew bent double with laughter. They had decided to play a trick on me and refrain from pulling the lever that would allow the backdrop to open on cue. There's not a lot you can do when you are trapped on stage and at the mercy of the stage manager!

Prior to one performance, an actor, who shall remain nameless, and no, it wasn't me, had partaken of quite a heavy liquid lunch, and decided to rest against a column on the side of the stage while he recovered from a sore head! Unfortunately, this caused him to disappear into the orchestra pit. I don't think that anyone really noticed, not from the audience side any way! He then reappeared downstairs looking rather dishevelled and shocked following his unplanned departure from the stage.

Then there was the time that a letter was supposedly sent to the stage manager demanding to know why the only people having a good time were those on the stage. Apparently the cast had been caught laughing continuously during a performance. I never did discover if the letter was true or not, but I think it the stage manager trying to assert some power over us. He also called an extra rehearsal and ran us all ragged!

Thankfully we never did hear another word from the management and we continued to laugh and enjoy ourselves on stage. It seemed the right thing to do, because let's face it, a pantomime is supposed to make people happy and have fun. The kids certainly made enough noise and their revelry was a joy to listen to.

I was asked only the other day why I have never appeared in more pantomimes. The truth is I was always working at Christmas, so I only ever did two pantos. The other being *Aladdin* in Norwich.

Released in America in March 1965, and in the UK in April 1965, *Be My Guest* was a film I made with David Hemmings. I played the role of Jim Matthews, while the other roles were played by a fantastic cast that included Steve Marriott, John Pike and Joyce Blair. Even the legendary Jerry Lee Lewis made an appearance!

We all used to sit in the make-up room playing poker for considerable amounts of cash after filming each night. Steve would not sit at the table. He used to spread himself out on the floor, sing the blues and play his mouth organ instead. All he wanted to be was a rock star. Actually I'm wrong, he just wanted to sing and perform on stage with like-minded musicians. It was his dream. Sometimes he would casually throw a fiver into the pot and say: 'I would have lost that anyway,' and keep on playing.

Then one day we all seemed to grow up. Steve became a rock star, David made the film *Blow Up,* and, for a time at least, was married to the American actress Gayle Hunnicutt. We still managed to find the time to meet up to play poker and drink in not the most reputable of places, with not the most reputable of people.

I watched a DVD copy of *Be My Guest* last year. I couldn't helping thinking that David Hemmings, Steve Marriott and myself all looked so young and respectable! Seeing it again also reminded me that Joyce Blair singing and shaking her famous hips made it a must-see 'B' movie back in the day.

As mentioned, my mother passed away when I was sixteen. I think the combination of so much work and losing Mum made me feel it was time to do something else. I felt completely lost and reasoned that travelling was the answer. That's probably why I eventually found myself in Kenya, having travelled through the Suez Canal on one of the Lloyd Triestino ocean liners.

Later, I travelled to Nairobi to meet a man called Tony Turner. As well as being part of my father's collection of reprobates, Tony was an avid chess, poker and bridge player, and lived life to its fullest. There were rumours that he had been the only conscientious objector during World War Two to avoid prison. As I say, this was a rumour and I cannot say it was a fact. Either way, he was the most interesting of men.

Tony and I arranged to meet at the Thorn Tree Restaurant, which, at that time, was the cafe located outside the New Stanley Hotel. This was situated in the dead centre of Nairobi. He informed me that he would walk through the restaurant carrying a copy of *The Times* under one arm so I would instantly know that it was him. Had I been told in advance that Tony was bald and under 5 ft. 1, not portly, though not slim, and would be wearing strange looking shorts and a bright shirt, I might have been less inclined to nearly fall of my chair in hysterical laughter! Fortunately, I managed to control my mirth and we became staunch friends.

I went on to stay with Tony, and his then wife, for quite a long time. He very kindly offered me the use of one of his Mercedes and his home as my base in Kenya for as long as I wished.

I will never forget arriving back at Tony's house on Kitisuru Road by car one night. I quickly became aware that Tony's two German Shepherds were making a lot of noise from inside the house at one of the night watchman's dog which was sitting on the veranda. It was only after I was half-way to the veranda that I realised that it wasn't a dog that was wagging his tail at me – it was a fully-grown leopard! All of a sudden my heart stood still. I have no idea what went through my mind except that I was too far from the car and not near enough to the house to get to safety. It seemed as if the little actor, who had played on Broadway at the tender age of fourteen, was about to become a fatal casualty before his twentieth birthday was even in sight! Then, to my great relief, I heard a voice shout: 'Go chui, go, go chui, go'. This was followed by five large and very unkempt dogs appearing on the end of chains making such a racket that the leopard up and left with a disdainful look at his aggressors.

'Jambo Bwana, everything alright now,' said the night guard, who had appeared seemingly from no-where. 'You go in.'

I nodded gratefully and then walked to the house.

This was not my last encounter with leopards. I think they are quite the most frightening of the big cats – that is my opinion and I stand by it very firmly!

Africa is a great leveller and when you stand with your back facing Nairobi, and your face pointing out over the beginning of the rift valley, you suddenly realise just how small and very insignificant you really are. When I travelled to Naivasha, a market town which is situated north-west of Nairobi, I saw the most incredible flocks of flamingos gracing Lake Naivasha. Their well-marked white and red bodies and flight paths as they glide onto the water is so magical. It's as if a pink hue is floating downward and taking over the water that houses so much wildlife. It's definitely one of nature's great wonders.

Africa was a time of personal repair, and probably one of the most invigorating twelve months of my life. I played in poker games that I had no right to be in, and spent time with legends of the great white hunter world. I sat and listened to stories of how some of the hunters had been mauled by lions because their clients had not followed the simplest of rules. But it was usually the white hunter who got hurt rectifying the clients mistakes!

Being out in the bush, and shooting for the pot, allowed one the opportunity to see wildlife from a totally different perspective. There were times when I thought I was alone only to realise that there was a man, with his leg curled around a tall walking stick more like a pole, just watching me with an expressionless face! Then without warning he would disappear and never to be seen again.

There was one occasion when I became aware that a few baboons were walking quite close to me. Someone once told me that where there are baboons, there are usually leopards, so I slowly made my way back to the Land Rover. My imagination was working overtime, and I kept thinking that I could hear the rasping sound that a leopard makes as it pads along. Luckily, I was wrong!

I met so many characters out there. For example, there was a rather rotund intellectual who, instead of going to Vietnam, accepted a job with the peace core teaching small smiley faced African children way out in the bush. He was actually based in Uganda. It was this peace worker who introduced me to Warragi, a locally made gin that, I am told nowadays, is an epidemic as far as local alcoholics are concerned!

Uganda is also where I also spent time playing golf in Iganga on the edge of the White Nile. It was there that I had to give way to hippos returning to the water. Take my advice, never stand between a dry hippo and a wet river, it can only end one way, and that is hippo one, golfer nil!

Just over a year later I was back in England, the red dust of the African roads was far behind me and once again a brand new phase in my life started to unfurl.

Following my return to London, I spent some time working as a window dresser in a department store in Oxford Street. I have no idea why I did that job, except that the family who owned the store were very old friends of my father. I think it was his attempt to try and get me back into a normal life. It didn't work!

The famous Carnaby Street in London was, by this time, in full swing and in truth probably getting close to being old hat. It was still buzzing, but it was now much more of a tourist attraction.

I had returned from East Africa not really sure if I wanted to carry on with my career as an actor. Despite the credits I had achieved to date, I was seriously contemplating going back to Africa. Still unsure of what to do with my future, I found myself being cast in individual episodes of both *Dixon of Dock Green* ('A

Quiet Sunday'), and *Softly Softly* ('Persistence'), in 1968 and 1969 respectively. I played shoe shop salesman in the former and something else of equally little importance in the latter. Then I found myself being cast in a film opposite Herbert Lom. For some reason, however, Lom pulled quit his role and the project was shelved. Thankfully, we all still got paid!

More excitingly, Frankie Avalon, Jill Haworth, Dennis Price, George Sewell, Richard O'Sullivan and Robert Raglan, who I later worked with in *Bless this House*, were just some of my colleagues in a horror film I appeared in. Produced by Tony Tenser, and directed by Michael Armstrong, *Horror House*, which was originally called *The Haunted House of Horror*, was quite an experience to be involved with. Made by Tigon British Film Productions, the film sees a group of teenagers visit a large house, said to be haunted, after becoming bored at a party. When one of the gang is killed in a knife attack, the rest attempt to solve the murder without police intervention.

Some of us stayed in an old hotel, which we also used for much of the filming. It appeared to have been built back to front, with the main entrance facing the sea. More of concern was the rumour that it was haunted. The rumour was that a very nasty set of events supposedly happened in the basement area of the building years ago. The story goes that a young maid met an untimely death at the hands of a gentleman, for want of a better word. The room where the maid is reputed to have lost her life had been bricked over. With the passing of time, many of the bricks had slowly started to fall away.

Some of the cast members, including me, decided to venture into the famous room as a dare. We soon noticed that the temperature was considerably colder in the room than the corridor outside. It was certainly a very unpleasant experience.

There was also an underground passageway to the little pub at the far end of the hotel. This is where Richard O'Sullivan and I, for some unknown reason, both ended up acquiring pet dogs. Richard's was a Shepherd type dog and mine was an English Pointer cross bitch. We both kept our pooches for many years. I later gave Vince Powell, one of our writer's on *Bless this House*, a puppy produced by my doggie. Unfortunately, he ate Vince's carpet and quite an amount of furniture before an allergy to carpet eating eventually instigated his demise. Nice dog, strange taste in food!

A lift in the hotel used to stop at certain floors and the whole ambiance of the place did not have the healthiest of atmospheres. It was a great setting for a horror film, but not the ideal place to have a holiday. None of us were sad to leave once the filming ended.

Incidentally, Richard O'Sullivan and I have stayed in touch. Just prior to writing this book, my wife and I visited him while we were staying in London.

In 1970, I went on location to Spain to play the Prince of Wales to Alec Guinness' King Charles I in the film, *Cromwell*. Being part of the production also gave me chance to rub shoulders with Richard Harris, Robert Morley, Dorothy Tutin, Frank Finlay and Timothy Dalton.

During the filming, a collection of us Cavaliers were facing Richard Harris as Cromwell. We, of course, were on the side of King Charles I – I had to be, as I played Sir Alec Guinness' son! A lovely actor called Robert Morley was also in the line-up. Robert was known mainly for his portly comedic roles and later in life for his devotion to good restaurants and fine fare.

He had been given a fairly small and slender Spanish horse as his mount. Most of the horses came from Medina's Stunt Stables just outside Madrid, and were incredibly versatile. I think Robert had been given this particular animal in order to make the process of mounting it a little less of a cumbersome affair. Unfortunately, in the line-up it looked as if he was on a toy rocking horse! Following a small conference, it was decided that a mound of earth should be built on top of which Robert and his horse were perched.

With the mound built and the veteran actor secured by the waist, or what one might call politely an ample-sized tummy, by a tight Spanish saddle, it was time to shoot the scene. The tension in the air was almost palpable as Irving Allen, the cigar-chomping producer of the film, mooched about looking stern. This extra hold up was worrying him as a good portion of the day had been lost.

'Action!' called director, Ken Hughes.

'I say,' piped up Robert. 'I don't know if anyone is interested, but we are no longer at the same height!'

'Cut!' shouted Ken.

'I think this could be due to the fact that my trusty steed is sinking,' Robert continued.

There was a slight pause and then everyone in the cast and crew fell about laughing. Well, all except Irving Allen who didn't see the funny side of the situation. He was last seen leaving the set for his mobile office in a flurry of frustrated smoke! By now, Morley's horse had sunk deep into its earth plinth and up to and past its knees. It was not the happiest of small Spanish horses. Robert, who was now quite close to the ground, was quickly removed from the poor horse.

Sir Alec Guinness' mount was an unbelievably magnificent animal who was worth a fortune. However, the horse had a hoof problem which meant that it was only really capable of standing and looking beautiful. He was unable to walk more than a few hundred metres due to a problem with the soles of his feet. Even a thirty second canter would induce a sudden and dramatic lameness.

Unaware of the horse's affliction, Sir Alec asked me very quietly as we walked about from the battle scene location.

'Robin, my dear boy,' said Sir Alec. 'Do you have any idea how one may stop this grand creature, if and when the opportunity ever arises?'

'Just gently pull back on the reins, Sir,' I confided. 'You will find he will stop and await your next command.'

'Ah,' replied Sir Alec. 'How very convenient'.

And that was the last that was ever mentioned about horses. Sir Alec was the master of the understatement, as many actors of overzealous performances would have discovered over the years, if they'd listened!

One of the sad things that happened during the filming of *Cromwell* involved an extra who signed an agreement in London that confirmed that he could ride a horse. Unfortunately, it failed to mention that not all of the horses were used to large explosions and massive smoke bombs, and other distractions that can happen on a battle field. And when his bolting horse speared him upwards and into space, he landed in such a way that he broke his back. He later discovered, while recovering in his hospital bed in Spain, that the film company had decided to relinquish any responsibility for his injuries. They argued that he obviously could not ride a horse as he had originally stated. I never did find out what became of him. Sad, but I suppose in the days of the so-called 'blood chits', it was unavoidable.

A stunt man on the film was also injured. This time it was at the studio back in England. An arc light fell on both him and his horse. I believe the man fared far better and received compensation from the company.

I was starting to wonder what, if anything, the acting world had in store for me, and this was making me restless. What I didn't realise at that time was that I was about to be offered a role that would change my life – forever!

Chapter Three

Enter Mike Abbott

'Robin, Thames TV want to see you at Teddington about a new series starring Sid James. They're interested in you playing his son.'

Hazel Malone

In this chapter, Robin describes how a call from his then agent, Hazel Malone, was eventually to see him cast in the quintessential family sitcom of the Seventies, Bless this House. *He also describes meeting Sid James for the first time, what happened during the rehearsal process and why each day working on the series was a learning curve.*

I picked up the phone and Hazel, my agent at the time, greeted me in her inimitable way. After the usual pleasantries were exchanged, Hazel quickly and professionally revealed her purpose for calling.

'Robin, Thames TV want to see you at Teddington about a new series starring Sid James,' she said. 'They're interested in you playing his son.'

Basically, all that meant was that a casting call had been put out, and my name had been accepted on the roll call. Agents always like to give you a bit of a boost. Well, they did in those days!

Thames TV had commenced broadcasting in July 1968, and by the time I went along to their Teddington base for my audition in 1970, the company was already turning out a host of popular programmes for their franchise area and the ITV network as a whole.

I was whisked into producer/director William G. Stewarts' office. At the time, Stewart was also riding high with the Patrick Cargill sitcom, *Father, Dear Father*. As well as being greeted by William – or William G. as he was known then – I came face-to-face with Sid James for the very first time. We talked for a while, read a scene or two from a script that was on Bill's table, and then I left. And that's basically all I can remember about my audition, except that Sid was very jovial and Bill was very fast and business like.

It wasn't long before I received another call from Hazel.

'Well, darling, that all went very well,' she said in her best theatrical voice. 'I'm pleased to tell you that you got the part of Mike Abbott, and rehearsals start very soon. I'll let you know more details soon. Get some rest, you'll be making twelve episodes back-to back.'

Before I could get as much as a single word in, Hazel had put down the phone and I was left with a dead line! The deal was done and dusted. She had worked out her ten percent, and I knew I had the job. So end of call and on to the next, which was her probably telling some poor bugger that they didn't get the job! It suddenly hit me, I was actually going to be appearing in a brand new series for Thames TV with Sid James – THE SID JAMES! So now I had two Dads to contend with! All I could think about was what Sid and Bill had said about the character of Mike Abbott – a character that both the public and I would soon come to know very well.

Fans have often asked me how Mike actually managed to live without a job. That's a very good question! Well, there was always food at home, together with a washing machine and Mum who fixed everything. His Dad who was good for a quick fiver, just to keep the peace. I think hand outs from his Dad seem to be Mike's only real income! The public must have taken note of this, because if I used a taxi when *Bless this House* was on air, the drivers often used say to me: 'Have you been borrowing off the old man again?' As all fans of the series know, Sid was essentially a struggling paper clip salesman, but somehow it never stopped Mike or Jean and Sally, for that matter, from going without anything thing, especially clothes.

I think Sid Abbott fondly considered Mike to be more animal and vegetable, than mineral – or even vaguely human! He was every father's nightmare! But when problems arose, Sally always came to his rescue and defended him. There's no doubt that Mike had a great life! And when things got a bit of a drag for him, there was always a cause to fight for!

Mike was not too hard to write for once his character had been hung drawn and quartered, so to speak. It could be argued that there were times when he just resembled a hairy thing on legs that made the occasional guttural noise. Although I don't think that's quite true or fair. There was a little pathos with the Mike Abbott character. I hope I played him in a way that still made him a likeable sort of bloke, and one that every mother could love. He meant no real harm to anyone, he just sort of was a loveable appendage that a lot of families have.

Playing a character that was younger than my real age was never a problem for me. I don't think that my brain has ever wanted to grow up anyway! Being the long-haired, strangely dressed art student of no fixed mental abode was just a joy. The complete lack of responsibility type character was easier to play than pulling a loo chain!

Right from the early days I used to think how much fun the art department must have had designing and making all of Mike's various weird and wonderful sculptures. It must have been the same for the wardrobe department when they were choosing my clothes and beads. But I was more than a little shocked to discover that they used to buy the beads I wore from a place in Knightsbridge for around seventy-five to eighty pounds! I couldn't believe how much money people were willing to spend on just wooden beads!

Going back to the day I first discovered I had been cast as Mike, I suddenly started to wonder whether the series would be a success. Would it run for more than one series? So many thoughts were racing through my mind that I decided to call Hazel back. By now she was able to tell me that Diana Coupland was playing my mother, and Sally Geeson was playing my sister. Wow what a cast!

I was later informed that Patsy Rowlands and Anthony Jackson would be playing the next door neighbours. Patsy was well-known for her many comedic roles, and was a great foil for any lead character to play against. She had already worked with Sid in *Carry On Loving* and briefly on *Carry On Henry*. Tony Jackson, the man with the expressive face and laugh to go with it, firmly believed in every line he was given and characterised it to the full. Tony appeared in a variety of theatre, radio and TV roles in his career. After *Bless this House* finished he continued to be popular after he was cast in the BBC children's show, *Rentaghost*.

Not long before *Bless this House* first began, Sid James appeared in *Two in Clover*, another sitcom made by Thames TV. It co-starred the late actor Victor Spinetti, and was, for my money, hysterical. Sadly, it didn't last more than one series. I don't know if that was ratings or personal agendas. All I remember is that

I thought that Sid and Victor on a farm was an excellent premise for a series.

Vince Powell, who created *Bless this House* with Harry Driver, later revealed how he'd suggested at a planning meeting that Sid should play a character that was married with a wife and family. Despite some disagreement from those present at the meeting, Sid concurred with Powell. With that, Sidney Abbott, a typical husband with an average wife and two kids, was born.

I personally think that *Bless this House* turned out to be the perfect vehicle to help move Sid away from the *Carry On* character that he'd developed. I think the bird-chasing character he portrayed in the much-loved saucy films had really come to the end of its life span. In fact, I would argue that *Bless this House* was a wonderful ending to a brilliant career.

In the early days of making *Bless this House* I lived with my then wife in a farmhouse in a place called Woollens Brook, which is situated close to Hertford Heath in Hertfordshire. It was the perfect example of the perfect English village with its cricket green slap bang in the middle, and its pub on the edge nearby. I divided a great deal of my drinking time between that pub and the one in Haileybury.

I later sold the farmhouse and spent the money indulging in my passion for horses. My neighbours, the Davis family, continued to ride with me through to the most beautiful bluebell wood imaginable on the way to the pub. Eventually a road was built through my gallops and a lot of the area was destroyed and has been lost to exhaust fumes and road rage, ho-hum!

I then made the decision to leave Woollens Brook and move back to London. Leaving the farm life was not the best move, but I did it anyway.

I have been told that the lovely old pub in Haileybury has since become a boutique boozer. I know it wouldn't feel the same if I returned. So in order to keep my memories intact, I shall continue to remember the area in my mind's eye.

I do remember with a lot of affection a man who used to live near to me in the area called Norman Sheffield. Norman played a large part in the beginning of the rock group Queen. He arranged for me to be at their first big concert in London, and I will never ever forget it. I also remember that his personal record collection was to die for! He has recently written a book – entitled *Life on Two Legs: Set the Record Straight* – which is a must-read for Queen fans, and those interested in those crazy times.

Going to work, for want of a better word, on *Bless this House* was just a joy. This is despite the fact that I was continually being beaten by the north circular and/or the foggy mornings trying to get from Hertford Heath to Barnet. Then, of course, I had to make my way to Hammersmith, before driving on to Teddington. It was sixty miles of sheer frustration, and that was before the electric system on one of my so called trusty cars would blow on the coldest mornings.

Sometimes I would travel to rehearsals with Diana. I would often listen to her reading out her lines and, more often than not, would be unable to stop laughing! She had great comic timing. She believed that everything she knew about comedy was learned from Sid.

My on-screen Mum had a thing about Citroen cars, and the standing joke was that you'd never be able to a rob a bank if you were driving her car as you had to wait for it rise up on its suspension before you could drive away! Even so, she was always on time. I seemed to be doomed when it came to getting myself to rehearsals. In sheer desperation, I started to use a hire car on a regular basis but I was still never on time – even without me at the wheel!

In the early days we rehearsed in a room at Thames TV, so it was never a strange place to be or to go to on recording days. But later, as Sally Geeson recalled in her foreword, rehearsals were moved to a nearby Scout hut. Our rehearsal room was always a good place to hear the best jokes or to fall asleep on well-placed mattress, especially if I'd been working in a theatre the night before!

We rehearsed from Tuesday morning until Saturday morning. William G. Stewart had every move, every blink of an eye lid in his head from the very first read-through each week. William's wonderful brain seemed to work in multi-camera mode all the time. He would take a pile of papers, fondly called a script, and turn it into something that made people laugh and cry all at the same time. William was a master at his craft, yet I always had a feeling that he would have loved to be on our side of the camera. He did, of course, eventually do just that with his Channel 4 quiz show, *Fifteen to One*, and, from what I heard, loved every minute of it!

On the Tuesday morning we would all sit down around a long table with Bill heading the chair. The whole cast for the episode would be there along with our script writers. We were like a merry band of vagabonds all waiting to see what the written word had in store for that week's episode.

Cups of tea, coffee, water or anything that made the voice purr out the words that our faithful writers had slaved over for us were consumed by the bucket load. Vince Powell, and in the early days, his writing partner, Harry Driver, obviously held a guiding hand without being intrusive to the other writers, such as Carla Lane and Myra Taylor. William G. and Sid would do quick and invaluable rewrites to the script. This would be done without a quibble or an objection as all the writers had total faith in them. Quite simply, Bill and Sid knew exactly what would work, and it always did!

Rehearsals were a never ending learning curve and it wasn't long before one realised that on the night Sid would be ten times as funny. This was in addition to being a hundred times as accurate with his timing and his manipulation of the audience's reactions to his comedic mastery. William G. once said in a TV documentary that he thought that Sid was a 'clever sod', and I agree!

Rehearsals were always a very strange time, especially the first day. For those not initiated with the way a studio sitcom is rehearsed, and how it all comes together, it can be quite a shock. There are no luxuries like doors or windows, the whole floor plan is made up of white sticky tape and the occasional piece of furniture, if one is very lucky. The way in which a door swings open or shut is shown by the direction in which the white tape is put on the floor. Getting from one set to another is easy, you walk through a white taped wall!

William G. plotted the whole of that week's episode from the floor plan and we, as the performers, only had to be in right place at the right time. The complexities of the director's job is the next step towards the finished product, a product that will make you stay on that channel or just switch over.

A coffee break would then follow the initial read-through. Being at the studio meant that everything was right there on hand. Bill, Sid and the writers would converse again on what needed to be done to make the various scenes flow. Then it was back to the table and another read-through.

The rehearsal room phone was an integral part of the morning procedure. Information from the occasional horse trainer was of major importance to more than one of the cast. Plus there was everybody's own personal lives to be accounted for. These were the days before mobile phone, of course. It was probably a good thing as the temptation to message all and sundry during the times when you weren't speaking would have been just too easy. I used to get myself into enough trouble with the standard landline on the wall as it was!

Before long, Tuesday became Wednesday and all too soon it was Sunday – and that's when we moved down into the large Studio One. This studio was one of the best in the country. During Thames' ownership, it played host to a number of classic shows, especially sitcoms. These included *Man About the House*, *George and Mildred, Robin's Nest*, *Never the Twain* and *Fresh Fields*. I think it's so sad that the whole studio complex is to be demolished to make way for a residential development in a year or two. It's the destruction of history – TV history! I don't understand why the studio cannot stay open, especially as there is such a chronic lack of studio space in the London area. For something that has helped give so many people so much pleasure, to lose it seems nothing short of criminal.

Sundays started very early with tech. runs for the cast and crew. All this, of course, was followed by a full dress rehearsal. The weekend was an enormous test of endurance for everyone – especially Sid.

Then, just when you energy level might be lacking, the audience came in between 7pm and 7.30pm. Many of them travelled for miles and miles to watch an edition being taped. They queued outside in all weathers for up to an hour before finally being allowed into the studio.

One wonders how long the public waited to get tickets for the show. They loved Sid, and how could they not? He was a man who could creating a laugh that kept on building and building just by giving a wink and a double take. You would never see Sid on screen with his famous hat pulled down. It was always perched above his forehead so that his face was totally visible so you could see every line, every crack and crevice. Sid's face was his trade mark, and he used it to every advantage. I learnt so much from this man of many talents.

The wardrobe and make-up departments at Thames were unbelievable. They all became close mates. Even though we didn't live in each other's pockets, they probably knew more about all of us than anyone else! I remember the lovely costume department's Lyn Harvey was with us for many of the shows. I bet she could tell some tales! It was as if they were all comrades in crime. They did us all proud and I will always be in there debt for they made recording day move along with an air of complete professionalism. There was no fluster, no panic, they all knew their jobs inside out If only people realised just how hard all of the production team on *Bless this House* worked. The crew is the base line and without them there would have been nothing! I have always said this and I believe it with all my heart. So a huge thank you to all those people who made it possible for us to be good or bad. That last bit was up to us!

As soon as the audience was seated, Bill would commence his warm-up and introduce us all to the audience. The last person he would introduce was always Sid. He would then take over the proceedings and used to do deliver the following old joke to the audience. This used to help put them at ease – and in a good mood!

A little boy and a little girl are both sitting in the bath.

Little Girl: Here, look what you've got! Can I touch it?

Little Boy: No, you've broken yours of already!

The audience would crack up just because Sid laughs, and Bill used to use these moments to make his way to the gallery and his post for the recording. Then we would be all set to go! Sid, Diana, Sally and I would all look at each other and say 'Merde', a lovely little French word that said it all! We never said 'good luck' or 'have a good one', we just said 'Merde'!

Then the tape started rolling, the countdown began and then theme music started to play – another episode of *Bless this House* was underway!

The great adrenalin rush, and the unbelievable high that seemed to overtake my body the very second that Geoff Love's theme tune started to play, is something that has never left me! How can I best describe the feeling? It felt like I had been tied to a stake, someone had yelled out fire and all the guns in the world had gone off – but, somehow, all the bullets had all missed me! I was still alive, euphoric and feeling as if I could fly to the moon!

When the first scene started the audience would sit there and gave the impression that they were as one and united in waiting to see who would make the first mistake. It was a bit like the old days when people used to go to the circus just to see if the chap on the high wire would fall off and crash to the ground. Without fail, one of us always did make a mistake, and the audience loved it! Sid would laugh and Diana would look straight at the audience, and, with her big blue eyes flashing wildly, would say: 'It wasn't me, honest'. Sid sometimes used to look over at me and say: 'It must be him,' or just look at the audience and laugh. The floor manager would call places and off we'd go again!

There were times when we taped scenes in the kitchen set that I would write a word or a line in the butter. If Sid spotted me, he would wipe it clean, look at the audience and say: 'That's got him, he won't know what to say now!' and of course he would laugh. And when Sid laughed, the audience laughed!

The cameramen loved Sid, and so did the camera! It zoomed into his face and made you smile. He made the live audience feel as if they were all part of everything that happened on the night.

You would never have thought that Sid was tired, or that he had a care in the world. Many times he had rehearsed in the daytime all week at Thames before appearing on stage during the evening in the West End stage revue, *Carry On London*. Then he did two incredibly strenuous days in the studio from early morning until night. Despite this, he joked and laughed and gave the performance of a laugh time. But then, that's what this business is all about. The final performance, the end product – the show in all its glory.

On the recording night Sid was unbelievable. His magic was so infectious that we all seemed to step up to the mark and let him set the pace. It was as if he had picked us all up and thrown us into a great big pot that bubbled away with such infection that it was impossible to get left behind. He drove the scenes with an electric prod. And when something did go awry, or even fractionally off the mark, there was that face full of mirth and laughter pulling the audience in until we were ready to go again.

Sid did have a unique take on how to conserve his energies while filming which Diana once recalled in a video documentary. He told her that his idea of acting was to never stand if you can sit, and you never sat if you could lie down. Which probably explains why there were a large number of scenes where Sid was able to sit down or lie down!

Sid would greet every stage hand with a 'Hello Matey!' and a big grin. He always said 'Matey' to everyone because it prevented him from having to remember their name! Then he'd mention a horse that had run its race in the wrong direction! Not once did I ever see anyone look sad after exchanging pleasantries with Sid. It didn't matter what kind of mood he was in, he always made people feel special. This, by the way, did not mean that he suffered fools lightly. No, he just didn't rub their noses in the crap that they had created for themselves. He advised people in such a way that they never felt pressured.

With me, Sid could be unbelievably blunt, but always with my best interests at heart. He often would warn me of other people's intentions and always to protect and ensure that I would survive. If only some people knew how perceptive Sid was and how much he cared about his on-screen family. He saw all and imparted what he thought was necessary to keep us all safe, popular and together. I wish I had listened more intently.

When it came to the scenes I played with Sid, all I really had to do was act like a trampoline. If Sid went up, I went down, and vice versa. Everything relied upon Sid's reaction to our reactions. The firm rapport between us both on screen made the character's believable.

Incidentally, I have met a few actors over the years who are very fond of upstaging their fellow actors on stage or TV. But they would have never stood a chance with Sid! He knew just when someone was encroaching on his personal space, and then they got stopped right there and then without even knowing that it was happening.

I was always on a real high after we had finished recording a show and couldn't come down for hours. I could never just go home and go straight to sleep. I think most actors and actresses feel the same after they finish a performance of any kind. Sid would usually go home pretty much straight away after the recording. But I would go straight up to the bar at the studios, which overlooked the beautiful River Thames, for a drink or two – or three!

I can honestly say it was a real joy making *Bless this House*. The camaraderie and the feeling of belonging to something that was as secure as it possibly could be in this precarious profession was amazing. All this and we got paid too!

Chapter Four

Blessed With Memories

'I recall that Robin was extremely sweet to me. He was extraordinarily good-looking, so it wasn't hard to see why Pamela fell for him!'

Sue Holderness

Appearing in all sixty-five episodes of Bless this House *has left Robin with a host of memories. In this chapter, he recalls further experiences of making the series. From the stress of recording the first episode, taped while industrial action was taking place, to the indignity of being upstaged by two small monkeys with full bladders! Robin also mentions why a Christmas special of* Bless this House *never made its way onto our TV screens, and finally offers his explanation as to why he didn't join the cast of the spin-off film version made by Peter Rogers and Gerald Thomas.*

With excitement around Sid James' new TV series continuing to build, *TV Times* magazine heralded the arrival of *Bless this House* in an edition dated 28 January 1971. You must remember that playing a family man on TV was a new experience for Sid. Indeed, he was fresh from playing Henry VIII in *Carry On Henry*. Cleverly, the magazine compared the fictitious life of Sidney Abbott with the real home-life of Sidney James. Abbott had two teenage children, and at that time Sid had two teenage children – Stephen (17) and Susan (13). Sid and his real-life family were pictured in the magazine with their boxer dog, Butch.

Here's a copy of the editorial printed next to the listings for the first transmission date:

BLESS THIS HOUSE at 6.45

SIDNEY JAMES
DIANA COUPLAND
ROBIN STEWART
SALLY GEESON in

The Generation Gap

BY VINCE POWELL AND HARRY DRIVER

With Gay Soper

Ladies and gentleman: we give you the Abbott family. Just another group of people who find themselves – unfortunately, they sometimes think – related and, at the same time, divided by their ever-present generation gap. In the chair at the top of the table is Sid: father, breadwinner and a representative of a stationery firm. Sid's interests in life are alphabetical – Ale, Birds Chelsea. He likes to think he's with it, but, in fact, he wouldn't know it if he saw it!

Then there's Jean, Sid's wife, enjoying the constant the constant battle of the sexes, particularly as she usually wins. Joining in, and often starting the confusion, are Sid and Jean's offspring, Mike and Sally.

Mike's just left college, but he's fat too busy straightening out the affairs of the world to bother about finding a job. Sally's in her last year at grammar school and is Daddy's little girl – or so Daddy thinks…

The Abbott family live in a state of perpetual turmoil, varying between hysterical neutrality, punctured with occasional moments of veiled hostility and open warfare.

Sid Abbott	Sidney James
Jean Abbott	Diana Coupland
Mike Abbott	Robin Stewart
Sally Abbott	Sally Geeson
Angela	Gay Soper

DESIGNER NORMAN GARWOOD
DIRECTOR/PRODUCER WILLIAM G.STEWART

Thames Television production

My abiding memory of making the first episode of *Bless this House* is that it was very stressful. None of us was nervous, as such. We were more apprehensive of the public reaction.

The very first episode of *Bless this House* was broadcast on 2 February 1971. However, this, and a further six episodes of the first twelve episodes, were taped in black & white owing to 'The Colour Strike', which took place from 13 November 1970 to 8 February 1971. This industrial action took place at all ITV regional companies, including Thames. Basically, technicians refused to use the new colour TV equipment until their pay dispute was resolved.

So there we were, a brand new series, a family show the like of which Sid had never done before – but in monochrome! Thankfully, there were enough Sid James fans, and other viewers, interested and we came through practically unscathed – well almost!

You may remember that in the first episode of *Bless this House*, Sally decided to wind Sid up by putting two novelty tomato ketchup squeezers under her sweater.

This gave Sid the opportunity to give one of his memorable double takes before ordering their removal. It was all good, clean fun and the viewers loved this sequence. That is all except for a certain Mary Whitehouse, who, for some reason, decided to criticise this part of the episode.

Despite Whitehouse's concerns, we continued to be beamed out in black and white until the normal service had been resumed, by which time it was obvious that *Bless this House* was set to have a long run!

Although running until 1976, the series was in the Top Twenty programmes from 1971 – 1975:

Top Twenty
Homes (Millions)

1971

5. Bless This House ITV 8.9
1972

15. Bless This House ITV 8.1

1973

9. Bless This House ITV 8.2

1974

4. Bless This House ITV 9.0

1975

15. Bless This House ITV 8.7

The series followed a tradition of sitcom production in this country. It didn't rip up the rule book or try to be different or clever. I think this is one of the reasons why it was so successful and continues to be loved to this day. I think that the English sitcoms of the time were so successful because they did not just rely on funny one liners. They featured more real situations that transpired and came together in such a way that it was funny without being intrusive. It was the difference that made the English approach to humour stand out in such a distinctive way. And we didn't have to swear to be funny!

It seems incredible when you think about it, but the main cast always managed to get on with each other. This was not an easy feat given the involvement of the press and petty jealousies. I must admit that I've heard embellished rumours of differences of opinion between the cast. As I am sure you know, if anything is successful, there is always someone who will try to destroy it. Over the years I have learnt that the easiest way to combat that kind of pettiness is to just ignore it. As with most rumours, they eventually die a natural death. We were a happy cast and I think that comes across on screen. I can clearly remember that when I was hosting a telethon for a New Zealand TV channel some years later, Diana came over and we reminisced about the series well into the small hours.

Diana and I did have one concern, though – Sid's health. Sid was a true workaholic and was never happier than when he was working. Mark you, I saw him even happier when a horse he had taken a small punt on actually beat the odds and romped home, but that's another story!

It's fair to say that what Sally and I remember about the *Bless this House* days is often quite different. For instance, sometimes I used to think that there wasn't really much for my character to do on certain episodes. Still, I guess even in a normal household the whole family doesn't live in each other's pockets 24/7. But somehow it all knitted together in the end and made sense.

Unsung heroes – that's what I call all of the various people who joined the main cast on most weeks. They were character actors who were members of a sort of an unofficial Thames TV repertory company. They could play just about anything that was asked of them. But their real value to the show, and to the casting director/s, was their unique idiosyncrasies. They were the straight men and women of the show, who ultimately helped to instigate the laughter. It was a joy to see some of the regular faces turn up on read-through days.

One such actor to help us enhance our laughter was David Battley, who sadly died following a heart attack in 2003. One of the episodes that he appeared in was first broadcast on 12 March 1973 and called 'Watch The Birdie!' Mike had decided to start a portrait photography business in Sid's garage and David's character, Mr. Jones, had decided to come along and have a photo taken of his stuffed parrot. The lines that were written for David's character were already very funny. But without his comic timing and delivery, they could have easily fallen flat.

From the very first read-through of the episode on a Tuesday morning, we knew that we'd really struggle to keep a straight face, because when he delivered a line you couldn't help laughing. David was a lovely man to work with and to watch. Another memorable episode he appeared in was 'Freedom Is…' in which he played a tramp.

Then there was Terence Alexander, who played a wide-eyed doctor in an episode called 'Father's Day'. This was a good decade before he went on to play Charlie Hungerford in the BBC detective series, *Bergerac.* Here was another actor who was used to playing the straight man, but was also capable of creating more than a few laughs of his own. In his one and only episode, Terence proved to be a perfect foil for Sid.

Remember the late, great Arthur English? He really came to public prominence when he took part in the BBC radio series, *Variety Bandbox*. Famed for playing a wartime spiv, Arthur only had to pull an expression and you laughed. Arguably, his biggest success on TV was when he played Mr. Harman in the Lloyd and Croft sitcom, *Are You Being Served?* In *Bless this House,* Arthur played a traffic warden in an episode called 'For Whom The Bell Tolls'.

My old pal Lionel Blair kept us all in stitches for the week when he appeared in an episode called 'Entente Not Quite Cordiale'. It was the only episode that saw Sid and Jean in a different country! The late, multi-talented actor, Ronnie Brody, also appeared in the same episode. His over characterised French accent, especially when he and Sid played were drunk, and toasting everything and anything at the drop of a hat, brought tears to my eyes. With Lionel Blair playing a sort of a wide boy from London, who danced with Sid as only Lionel could, all the ingredients were in the script, but they made it something extra special. The steadfast June Whitfield also graced us with her beauty and comic talent that same week.

Admirable performances also came from the likes of male supporting actors including John Clegg, James Appleby, the forever jovial Bernard Stone, Johnny

Wade, David Lander, Ivan Bevis, the always reliable Harry Littlewood, that powerful actor David Bauer, Norman Chappell, Richard Fraser, Donald Morley, James Coussins, Michael Logan, Robert Raglan, Roger Avon, Bill Pertwee, and that self-proclaimed charmer, the very good looking David Charkham. I could go and on!

We were also blessed with the presence of female supporting actors including Vivienne Cohen, Beryl Cooke, Marjorie Gresley, Stella Tanner, Sarah Maxwell and Barbara Evans.

Juliet Harmer also made a memorable appearance as a new neighbour in an episode called 'The Day Of Rest'. I seem to recall she got quite attached to one of my bizarre sculptures called 'Frontal Nude Protesting'!

Then, of course, there was the stunning Vanda Godsel, who played my busty and ever understanding art teacher. She managed to wind Sid Abbott around her little finger in an episode called 'Tea For Two And Four For Tea'.

A special mention should be made to Peggy-Ann Clifford, who, incidentally, never allowed any illness she had to come between her and a performance.

Gay Soper played a slightly dizzy blonde in two episodes of the series. If you watch these episodes now you can see how well Gay and Sid both worked together.

I was delighted when Gay agreed to share some of her *Bless this House* memories with me for this book:

> Gay: I recall that the director, William G. Stewart, told me that he decided to give me the role of Angela "Hotpants", an "artist's model", after seeing me walk across the courtyard to the audition room! I think in those days I walked with a bit of a Marilyn Monroe

wiggle and it was evidently just what he wanted for the part in the first episode of the series.

I remember everyone being extremely friendly and welcoming. Robin was very cheery, bright, and wisecracking; Sally was sweet, and what a thrill it was to meet and do scenes with the inimitable Sid James, who was as full of good humour and roguish twinkling eyes as I had hoped he would be.

It was simply a joy to do that first episode, and even nicer to do the second one, in which I played a short sighted barmaid who kept losing her glasses. I felt completely at home and altogether I have very, very happy memories of the entire programme and all involved with it.

Sue Holderness also recalls the week she spent with us all on *Bless this House* with great affection:

Sue: Thinking about my short time on *Bless this House* brought back some very happy memories. I was so excited to be offered the role of Pamela Huntley-Johnson, the short-lived fiancée of Mike Abbott, in 'The Bells Are Ringing'.

Going into an established sitcom as a guest artiste can be a very unnerving experience, but I remember everyone being very welcoming and helpful. Robin was extremely sweet to me. He was extraordinarily good-looking, so wasn't hard to see why Pamela fell for him!

It was a real thrill to discover that I would have a small scene with Sid James, who had always been a great favourite in our house – he did have the most infectious, filthy laugh! Another bonus for me was that I had a scene with the wonderful Windsor Davies, which I boasted about when he became a household name in *It Ain't Half Hot Mum*! My big regret was that Mike (Robin) and I didn't actually have a scene together – even though we were supposed to be engaged!

I'm not sure why I was offered the role, but a couple of years before, I did a children's series entitled *Tightrope* in which I played Joanna Barrington-Smythe, another very posh bird. Maybe William G. Stewart spotted me in that programme and kept me in mind?

I returned to Thames in Teddington in 1983 to make an extremely funny series called *It Takes a Worried Man*, playing a middle class girl called Liz (girlfriend of the worried man of the title). But, of course, it was in 1984 that I got my big break playing Marlene (there was nothing posh about Marlene!) in *Only Fools and Horses*. *Only Fools* was made at BBC Television Centre, but when John Sullivan wrote the spin-off series, *The Green Green Grass*, we taped it in the same studio at Teddington Studios where I taped my episode of *Bless this House*. It felt like coming home!

I'm sorry I didn't know at the time about Robin's passion for horses – a passion that I share. And I'm sorry too that our paths crossed so briefly.

Many of the episodes of *Bless this House* included required supporting artistes. One such artiste was Melinda Jackson:

Melinda: Working as an extra on *Bless this House* was such fun. I wish we could get those days back again.

Robin was lovely he spoke to everyone, including the extras. He didn't act like a star, although, of course, he was. I remember he treated us like equals and was so nice.

There is one actor who I haven't mentioned so far. His name is Robin Askwith. You may recall that as well as appearing in an episode of *Bless this House* entitled 'A Touch Of The Unknown', Askwith also appeared in the spin-off film version of the series. For me, it was a bit of strange experience knowing that a film was being made and I wouldn't be part of it. Many people have asked me why I didn't play Mike Abbott on the Big Screen. Well, contrary to what you may have read, the reason was that I had already signed to appear in a play in Bournemouth. Sid and I discussed the situation at great length. He made it perfectly clear that he really didn't think it was that important as he didn't like sitcom spin-off films. It was, of course, made by the people behind the *Carry On* films, and so taking part in the *Bless this House* film was, I believe, part of his contract with them. The funny thing was that Askwith and I shared the same agent at the time. This meant that good old Hazel Malone didn't miss out on any commission! I believe they all had a good time making the movie, and that my old mate Askwith played a very cool and groovy (not to mention blonde!) version of Mike Abbott.

It has been a number of years since Robin Askwith and I last saw each other. I believe it was when he was touring in Australia, and I was living and working down under. Who knows, maybe our paths will cross again one day at a memorabilia fair or a similar type of event?!

Anthony Jackson was also not part of the film. Instead, the role of Trevor was played by *Carry On* film regular Peter Butterworth. I believe Anthony was also appearing in a play at the time. There was certainly nothing sinister about it at all.

Life went on at the same pace for the original cast. Sally was Sally, Diana was Diana and Sid continued to try to back a winner! As for me? Well, unfortunately my problems with cars, frost and the north circular didn't change. I continued to be late for rehearsals, but usually only by a few minutes. Again, this is something which has been totally blown out of proportion as time has gone on!

On the subject of old rumours, I did once read that I supposedly spent some of my time inebriated on the set of *Bless this House*. This is completely untrue. Besides, I don't think I would have lasted the full run of the series if I had been!

As I'm sure you know, the *Carry On* films were produced by Peter Rogers and directed by Gerald Thomas. I can't be sure, but I think that I might have met one of them at a party in Beaconsfield long before the iconic film series started.

The *Carry On* team was very special, and they all jelled together in their own way. I was never asked to appear in one or more of the films, in case you were wondering, but then I really don't think I would have fitted into their long-established set-up. Sally Geeson, however, fitted into the series perfectly.

I would argue that one of the appeals of *Bless this House* for the viewers was that life in the Abbott household was never boring! There was always something to keep the laughter bubbling along. Sid Abbott's life was a merry-go-round of mishaps and family intrigue.

Writer Carla Lane was instrumental in making life for the Abbott's as chaotic and as funny as possible. Carla had a way of writing episodes that made them both a joy to read and perform. In the early days she co-wrote equally funny episodes with her then writing partner, Myra Taylor. Carla was not just a writer of funny lines, she knew how to create scenes that featured pathos too. I am so pleased that she went on to have even bigger success with sitcoms like *Butterflies* and *Bread.* I am sure Sid would also have been over the moon!

I was really delighted when Carla agreed to recall the days she wrote for *Bless this House* in this book:

> Carla: *Bless this House* was a very enjoyable time for me. I was a new writer so it should have been a scary experience, but they made it easy to get through. It was the first time people said I was clever. I wasn't very good at school. The teachers liked me, but I just wasn't very good at the work. So, in a way, working on the series was a bit like my schooling.
>
> Robin was pleasant, always pleasant, and Sid was wonderful to work with. He was a nice man, very appreciative. There was a softness about him. But then I have always been lucky with the actors I've worked with. Sid was very serious about his work. Everything had to be just right. If he liked a line, he would really laugh, and then you knew that he was pleased.
>
> I wrote a total of fifteen episodes with Myra Taylor, I loved her company but I eventually decided that I wanted to write on my own. In fact, I did end up writing ten episodes for the series alone.
>
> I always went to the recordings of *Bless this House*, as with all of my programmes in my career. I always needed to see that it was right.
>
> They were good days and I really learned what made people laugh working on that series.

Bless you, Carla, for presenting script after script after script that made us all laugh our way through the read-throughs, and all the way to recording day. All of the writers that were involved with *Bless this House* somehow seemed to know that if you wrote for the master, Sid, then everything else would just fall into place.

There is an old saying in our illustrious business – Never work with children or animals! When I appeared in *Camelot*, Sir Pellinore, King Arthur's trusty friend, had an old English sheep dog that used to slowly plod on to the stage each show. Invariably, his big fluffy coat would become unbelievably hot, and in no time, as the lights were ferocious, he would just lie down on the floor and pant looking very stately and quiet and regal. Well, as much as an old English sheep dog could look on a Broadway stage! Another problem was that he never had his nails cut. He was always taken to Central Park by car for his daily walks, so his toe nails never got worn down on the pavement. Consequently, when it was time for him to stand up from his sprawled position on the stage, he would slip and slide about and poor old Sir Pellinore would always mutter very audibly: 'He's been on the ale again!' This brought much laughter from the audience and the old English sheep dog kept his dignity, even though he stole the scene without even trying.

I can personally recall being upstaged by more than one animal when we were taping an episode of *Bless this House called* 'If The Dog Collar Fits'! We had some Marmoset monkeys on that particular show and Sally decided that they should be rewarded with treats all day long. She gave them a never-ending supply of juicy green grapes every time she visited them in the props room.

The episode that night had been going well. We reached the last scene of the night and it was almost time for me to bring on the monkeys. As you can imagine, a tiny monkey's tummy can only carry so much green grape juice, so there was a bit of a disaster when I walked onto the set. With the tape rolling, both monkeys, holding their maleness between first and forefinger, decided to spray my shirt and anything else that the offending liquid explosion could reach! The audience loved it and the monkey's screeched with delight. William G., however, was not amused. He was worried about the extra overtime that would need to be paid to the crew as there would have to be a studio wait while I got changed. I didn't care, I had been left dripping wet and smelling not exactly as sweet as a rose! Sid was roaring with laughter and Sally was politely grinning away as she said things like: 'Oh Robin, it couldn't have been the grapes, could it? Diana was equally amused!

Thanks to wardrobe, I got a fresh change of clothes and I was back on set in next to no time. I think if I had gone to the monkey enclosure at London Zoo that particular night, I would have been more that popular. I will let you all work that one out!

I have to admit that working with animals on the show was a lot of fun, even if they did steal most of the scenes that they were in. Our budgie stole many a laugh, whether it was hanging upside down mimicking death, or simply kissing his mirror. Although, I think you would have to agree it takes more than a tweety bird to upstage Sid James!

Our dear, sweet, little budgie, who lived peacefully in the props room all week, as far as I know, and came out for the tech. run on Saturday and on the Sunday recording day. One week, the budgie managed to vacate its cage. It flew off into an area of the studio where the steel girders and a multitude of lights lived. Sadly, there was no possible way that anyone could retrieve him from his lofty new home.

The only other time that we had a budgie drama was when we were filming the picnic scene in the episode 'Never Again On Sunday'. Our little feathered friend just went absent without leave. To this day, I cannot for the life of me remember if we got him back or not! Between dogs, budgies stuffed and live parrots and full-bladdered monkeys, we certainly had our share of animal nightmares!

Animal problems were not just confined to our programme at Thames. I remember hearing that on one occasion Yootha Joyce, who was making *Man About the House* at the time, was stopped at the security gate by an over-zealous security guard. The guard had decided to not allow her much-loved and cherished pooch to enter the studios. Yootha, who did not suffer fools lightly, was, as you can imagine, not in the slightest bit impressed. The problem, however, was resolved when the head of light entertainment, Philip Jones, came down and had a quiet word with the security guard.

Thinking about all these animal problems reminds me of James Robertson Justice. You may remember that he used to play Sir Lancelot Spratt in the *Doctor* films. He used to sit in the dining room at Pinewood Studios with a large black crow sitting on his shoulder. This probably explains why he never had any guests sitting with him at lunchtime.

I was once invited to go to the opening night of a big circus that came to town in Townsville which is in the far north of Queensland. In those days they still had big cats and elephants and camels and other large animals.

The press were there in force and the circus owners grabbed me and plonked a lion cub into my arms. This particular cub was not the smallest pussy in the world and promptly wrapped his paws around my neck. He held on with each and every claw that it owned while I tried to keep smiling. The picture, which ended up in the paper, still looks terrific. Well, if you don't look too closely at my face which was just a little strained. I decided there and then that running away to join a circus was not quite my idea of the perfect life!

When people ask me what is my favourite food, I can reply instantly. But if anyone asks me what is my favourite episode of *Bless this House*, then I simply can't think of just one. For me, they all have their own charm, even those I wasn't in as much as the others! The whole series was such a joy to be involved with. I can confirm that Sid's personal favourite episode was 'The Frozen Limit'.

Lots of people have said to me over the years that they considered the episode 'The Long Distance Walker' to be their favourite. I never quite understood what the fascination was with Linda Skoog, who played Lesley, and the road walk scenes until I watched it again recently! I realise now that 99% of those people who told me it was their favourite episode were actually male. I guess it wasn't just Sid and Trevor slowly falling apart in the sponsored walk scenes that captured the viewer's attention! No, it was Leena's in those little white shorts swaggering along the road!

On the subject of that particular episode, Sid fans might be interested to read that the walk scenes were filmed very close to his home, which was not far from Pinewood Studios in Buckinghamshire.

People have often asked me why we never made a Christmas special of *Bless this House*. I think it would have taken away some of the magic a bit if we had. Let's face it, our script writers already had plenty of great situations to play with. I think it was just as well that we left obvious turkey burning, tree falling over and Sid in a silly hat gags well and truly alone. Also, our various busy schedules meant it would have been too difficult to have made a Christmas special as well.

Many people have also asked me if Sid, Diana, Sally and I socialised together. To be honest, apart from eating together at the studio, we didn't socialise that much away from work. We had a few meals at Sid and Val's place, and every now and then I would see Sid at a function. To be honest, we kept our family very much a studio affair. Vince Powell once sad how similar we were to a real family when we sat eating together in the restaurant at Thames.

We never really had a big end of series party as such. I think we all had the next gig to go on to. If we did have a get-together, it was usually quite informal and held at Sid's house.

TV Times magazine once paid for both Sally and I to go to Rabat in Morocco for a couple of weeks to stay in the incredible resort. We both did a photo shoot in the desert wearing the most outrageous clothes of many, many colours! We got to see beaches that seemed to stretch as far as the eye could see. There was also time to play with horses in the desert, laze by the pool and play tennis in the courts in town. Amusingly, a copy of the magazine feature, by Jill Whiffing, turned up on the internet recently. The feature started as follows:

> Robin Stewart, the son in *Bless this House*, talks the way he looks: slick, speedy and smart. His rapid chatter, apparently off the top of his head, shows that he has considerable clothes sense.

Here are just a few of my quotes which the *TV Times* printed above a large black & white photo – taken by Ron McFarlane – of me with Sally Geeson, as we posed on the Plage des Nations in the scorching heat of Morocco:

> If you sneak into a place and you're sort of a humble and meek and you're wearing all these incredible colours, the colours are going to detract from you anyway. You've always got to beat what you're wearing, but you must do it with subtlety. You've got to have the confidence to pull it off.
>
> One thing I can't carry off, in town, is one of those incredible djellaba (like caftans) during the day. It's a pity, really, because they're the coolest things to wear when the old currant bun is beating down. The Arabs have been wearing them for centuries – which must prove something. I think the bowler hat brigade should leave off their heavy gear and get into caftans for the office. I'm sure they'd be a lot happier for it.
>
> The white suit with butterflies and flowers is one of my favourites. It's not really suitable for wearing on London buses, because if you get a speck of dirt on it you're done for, but it's marvellous for tripping across the beach in the sun. I don't really give a damn about fashion. I wear what I want to and as far as I am concerned that's where it's at.

While there, I struck up a friendship with the chief of police and shared some amazing dinners with him. He took me into the Souk and showed me how the young pick-pockets worked the tourists.

Sally and I also went to the Souk together and had a great time. I stayed on and went to Marrakesh and across the Andes to Ouarzazate after Sally returned to

London. Incidentally, Ouarzazate has often been used as a location for various films. These have included *Star Wars* and *Gladiator*.

I had the unique experience of meeting the Blue Men when they came in to town. The Blue Men are so called because of the blue dye that they add to their clothing. They arrived on camels and horses and set up an enormous camp. They had camel fights, ram battles and set up a traveling market. Then they left as quickly as they arrived and the streets were empty again. Now there's an airport, a Holiday Inn and it's a big tourist resort. But in the early Seventies the area was so much different, it was wild and untamed.

Out in the desert, in the middle of nowhere, there with a number of strange buildings seemingly made of stone and marble. I still have photographs of a solitary child sitting outside a small mud-type building looking out to nowhere, while his father made pots on a wheel.

Thinking of this visit reminds me that there was a hotel in the middle of absolutely nowhere with a guard posted outside in a sort of a sentry box. There was another sentry type box situated close by. Inside there was an eagle and on his leg was a light chain. When you politely asked the guard a question, the bird would look at you with his head cocked to one side. The light chain allowed the eagle just enough freedom to reach the guard. It made you feel as if you didn't really belong.

Words cannot express how grateful I am that people still remember, discover and enjoy *Bless this House*. I continue to receive numerous letters, emails and messages from fans of the show. I find it such an incredible experience to read that something that we all did so long ago continues to be loved by so many people. I know that Sally is just blown away when people come up to her out of the blue and say how much they enjoyed the series and watching us all. As I write, Sally is on board a cruise ship entertaining fans and travellers alike, and recalling the days when she was one of the Abbott family. We're both so lucky to still be here to experience its continued success. I only wish Sid, Diana, Anthony and Patsy were here to bask in all the continued glory too.

Diana used to receive mail from parents asking how she coped with Mike and Sally as her children. Lots of people seemed to get totally wrapped up in the Abbott family. This is usually the kind of thing that tends to happen with soap opera actors rather than those appearing in a sitcom. I found it really quite strange that people actually thought that Diana was our real Mum! I don't think that Diana minded too much. I think she took it as a compliment on her performance as Jean.

I still can't get over how much *Bless this House* changed my life. I still get messages from women (and men!) saying that they fancied me back in the day. I never saw myself as being a pin-up, and so you can imagine the shock I had when, low and behold, there I was in the centre pages of magazines and newspapers looking either sultry or apparently a little sexy. Then there were the photographs of Julie Ege and myself striding through Heathrow Airport looking like two Hollywood stars around the time I made a film with her. There were even photos printed of me riding large horses and looking very romantic in strange and exotic places. Strangely enough it didn't seem to have a transition stage, so it quickly became the norm.

Thanks to the internet, I have been able to keep in contact with a number of friends who I first got to know back in the days of *Bless this House*. One such friend is the actress, Françoise Pascal. Many readers will remember Françoise from her days playing Danielle Favre in the LWT sitcom, *Mind Your Language*. I was very flattered by her reminiscences of our very first meeting:

> Françoise: Meeting Robin was the highlight of my life! I met him at Thames TV whilst I was doing a show for Vince Powell. I think Robin was having lunch with some TV executives, I am not too sure, but he had met Vince in the bar of the TV station. I went to meet him as I was working on one of his shows called *Rule Britannia*. Vince and I talked about my career in TV. He could not believe his luck that I was doing a TV show for him because he thought I was a movie star! While were talking, Robin walked in the room and sat with us. Well, I almost fainted as he was the most gorgeous man I had ever seen! I felt all goose pimply when I met him and was smitten at first sight. I could not say anything, he was so chatty and so very charming and oh those eyes! I thought that he could have played a very younger version of Richard Johnson in films as he was that handsome. I admit that I left the studio feeling totally elated!

I have so much to thank Sid James for. But unfortunately I never found the right time to be able to thank him to his face when he was alive. I just hope that wherever he is now he knows how grateful I continue to be.

Chapter Five

Beyond Bless this House

'Robs, tell the second assistant that the camera crew are getting burnt by the flames.'

Julie Ege

As the production of Bless this House *didn't take up the whole year, the cast of the series were able to take on a variety of other acting roles and projects. So in this chapter Robin takes the opportunity to recollect the other theatre, film and TV productions he appeared in during the first part of the Seventies. From working with Wilfrid Brambell in a BBC drama, spending a summer season on the end of Bournemouth Pier with Benny Hill stooge, Henry McGee, and to travelling to Hong Kong to make the Hammer horror film,* The Legend of the 7 Golden Vampires, *with Peter Cushing and Julie Ege.*

When he wasn't recording episodes of *Bless this House*, Sid would take a Sam Cree farce on the road, such as *The Mating Season*, or make a *Carry On* film. Diana would spend time with her family and look at a drama, while Sally would appear in a film. I too was able to take advantage of the various roles that I was now being offered. One such role saw me playing Rembrandt's son, Titus, in a ninety-minute BBC drama which focused on the famous Dutch artist following the death of his wife. First broadcast in 1971, *Rembrandt* was made at BBC Television Centre. Richard Johnston played Rembrandt and Jill Bennett played Geertje. Also worthy of note is that the *Steptoe and Son* actor, Wilfrid Brambell, played Beggar Saul.

The one thing that has stuck in my memory about Wilfred Brambell is that it was always safer to stand up wind of him! Wilfrid would look at you, wink and then walk away. Before he had even taken a few steps the wind would hit you and settle. He could then be heard chuckling away.

Brambell became a fun person to have lunch with, and it would amaze me to watch him devour his favourite dish which, at that time, was moules marinière. Although I don't think that it was the moules that gave Wilfrid his gastronomic wind expulsions. It was more of the old cabbage variety. Wilfrid always seemed to get great amusement out of this small yet effective room clearing exercise! I say all this with the greatest of fondness as he was always most respectful to me and to any of the many luncheon guests that he entertained – with or without the wind!

In 1972 (commencing 16 May for the season), I appeared in *The Man Most Likely To* at the Pier Theatre in Bournemouth. The cast also included Henry McGee, Richard Davies, Jean Trend and Moira Foot. Incidentally, this is where I met my current, and last wife, who I married in 2012 on the beach in Coff's Harbour in Australia.

Then, in 1975, I toured in another farce with Henry and Deborah Watling, called *Two and Two Make Sex*. Venues on the tour included the Bristol Hippodrome, where one reviewer said that the production: 'Developed from a rather contrived start to a bubbling evening of situation humour'. They added that the funniest moments were when two scenes were acted simultaneously, and that it was brilliantly directed by Jack Watling, Deborah's father.

We even took this play to Ireland, and what a treat that was! I just love Cork because of its golf and its culture. There some great inns where the beer flows with the help of some of the best cellar men in the world. God bless them all!

Playing opposite Deborah was great fun. She was one of the few people I met who didn't allow success to go to her head. Debs had previously appeared in *Doctor Who*, and also played Cliff Richard's girlfriend in the film, *Take Me High*.

The lovely Sonia Fox also appeared in *Two and Two Make Sex*. Sonia had previously appeared in the ATV series, *Emergency Ward 10*, and later played Sheila Harvey in *Crossroads*. Both of these soaps captured the hearts of the viewing audience and created huge stars of all their performers.

I remember with great fondness playing opposite Henry McGee, who was for many years one of the regular cast members of *The Benny Hill Show*. He always had female co-stars who were not only good looking, but were talented professionals well-versed in their profession. In *The Man Most Likely To* there was the tall, leggy Moira Foot who trained at the Aida Foster School. She was much loved by the viewers as Cynthia in the LWT sitcom, *Doctor at Large*, and as Miss Thorpe, one of Mr. Rumbold's temporary secretaries, in *Are You Being Served?*

It might surprise you to know that I didn't guest on any TV chat shows during the making of *Bless this House*. All of the interviews I took part in were for newspapers and magazines. I was also required to take part in numerous interviews for local newspapers and radio stations when I was on tour. Then there were the afternoon croquet sessions with the vicar and his merry band of supporters, of which there were many. These were mostly ladies of the congregation, and they played a mean game of croquet beating me every time! I remember that the then Lady Mayoress of Yeovil was a great hostess on quite a few occasions. She always looked after the visiting actors with great panache. But then local dignitaries are just such an integral part of a tour as they always seem to come to ones rescue at just the right time. You end up spending the afternoon playing garden games and eating cakes and ice cream.

I was cast as Leyland Van Helsing in the 1974 horror film, *The Legend of the 7 Golden Vampires*. The title was a co-production between Hammer Films and Shaw Brothers and presented as a Hammer/Shaw Production. Interestingly, it turned out to be the last of Hammer's Dracula films.

Directed by the legendary Roy Ward Baker, the film also starred Peter Cushing, David Chiang and Julie Ege. An edited version of the film was released in North America with the title *The Seven Brothers Meet Dracula*. Another alternative title was *The Seven Brothers and Their One Sister Meet Dracula*.

To summarise, the film sees my character Leyland Van Helsing and a lady called Vanessa (Julie Ege) assist my father, vampire hunter Professor Van Helsing (Peter Cushing), and various local kung fu exponents rid a village in China in the 1900s of, yes, you guessed it, seven vampires! This is despite the arrival of Count Dracula (John Forbes-Robertson), who attempts to cause more than a little interference in the guise of a warlord.

Peter Cushing, Julie Ege and myself headed off to Hong Kong to make the film. At that time the unrivalled Shaw Brother had a monopoly on the movie market in China and Taiwan. They not only owned film studios outside Kowloon, but also owned a chain of cinemas. At any one time there would be over six movies being made at the Shaw Studios. I think they based their operation on the Hollywood system of the time as they created their own stars and had them tied up in unbreakable contracts.

Julie and I spent hours and hours at Delhi Airport on our way to Kowloon. I think we must have bet on every cockroach in the departure area as they frantically ran across the floor in search of a dropped morsel. It was with great relief that we arrived in Hong Kong and were driven to our hotel.

We were informed that there was to be a special banquet held that night in our honour. There were umpteen courses delivered to our tables and, much to Julie's shock horror, we were faced by a tiny monkey bound up in a small wicker basket. It was just too much. Warm monkey brains was one delicacy that we chose to avoid. Thankfully, this didn't cause any offence to our gracious hosts.

We were treated to such delicacies as boiled or roast chicken feet on our time at the studios in Kowloon. I am not quite sure which method of cooking was used as they arrived at the studio delivered by vendors on bicycles who had peddled for miles to sell their wares.

The various cafes in the studio grounds had an abundance of stray dogs floating around the tables. When one of the pups could not be spotted one afternoon, Julie, in all innocence, asked a waiter where they had all gone. She was more than a little shocked when a waiter pointed to the soup. We never did establish whether he was joking or not!

During the filming of one scene a camera had to track along a side of a trench that was on fire. This was designed to stop the zombies from attacking us.

'Robs, tell the second assistant that the camera crew are getting burnt by the flames,' said Julie.

I went over and spoke to the man in question.

‘Not to worry,’ he replied. ‘There are many more crew in the main building!’

Another scene in the film was shot at a lake. It was very cold there and even colder in the water! While we were in our trailer waiting to be called to go out to the lake, Julie thought it would be very funny to tie a great big red ribbon very tightly around my rapidly shrinking male member. The reason being that she didn’t want the camera crew to miss any ‘thing’ – no matter how small! I walked to the lake with the red bow still firmly attached to my manhood which amused the crew no end. All the same, I had my agent cut the scene from the film. Ironically, of course the red bow joke was very tame compared to what you can view on the internet these days!

While we were filming on the China border, the Milk Marketing Board sent out a crew from Australia to film both Julie and I drinking milk on the set. When Julie and I went to the premiere of the film in London, there was a section of the audience that roared with laughter when the advertisement was shown. Well, both of us were known for drinking spirits, and certainly not milk!

Filming on the China border also brought an unexpected opportunity – that of driving a Sherman tank! It was awesome experience, and not what I expected at all.

Having completed filming on *The Legend of the 7 Golden Vampires*, we flew back into Heathrow Airport on Christmas Eve. The following morning I paid a visit to a hospital in the East End of London to deliver the elderly patients a bar of Cadbury’s chocolate, a packet of tissues and a Christmas card. All these little presents were paid for by my fan club. It was run by a lady called Miss Ellis, who was an employee of one of the fashionable girly magazines of the time. She looked after so many people in the business, although mostly popular singers. Miss Ellis took no money for her work running the fan clubs, she did it purely out of love. As well as looking after all my fan mail, she wrote many articles about the various adventures I got up to.

Some of these very proud older folk did not have one visitor at Christmas, but they were still feisty. Believe me, I had to have my wits about me at all times, as some of these old ladies were as bright as brass tacks! Mind you, as soon as I offered to give the gifts to someone else they changed their tune. I always made sure they had the gifts safely in their hands before I moved to the next room for fear of getting an ear-bashing! I know that I did manage to leave a few smiles behind at the hospitals after my Santa Claus duties, so that made it all worthwhile.

I appeared on an episode of *Whodunnit?* in 1975. It was a highly-popular game show where viewers played detective at home, while a small audience panel and a team of celebrities in the studio attempted to solve a specially-filmed murder mystery.

Apart from the first series, when Edward Woodwood was the presenter, *Whodunnit?* was hosted by one-time Doctor Who, Jon Pertwee. I must admit I saw more of Jon in Ibiza than in England. This was before the little Spanish island become the place it is now. Back in those days it was just a really cool place to just chill, feel safe and party with friends. Somerset Maugham's nephew, Robin Maugham, had the most beautiful home in Ibiza. It was the same house where he hung a large and valuable Gainsborough picture on the dining room wall. That was until it was stolen in a robbery. The thieves came in from the sea and climbed up his private stairway on the cliff face and simply cut the painting out of its frame. Poor Robin eventually died lonely and a little desolate. He was a lovely man and a great raconteur. Unfortunately, he was also a devoted lover of the cocktail hour.

Anyway, back to the plot. I played opposite my old mate Steve Hodson in *Whodunnit?* Steve was very much a heart throb in those days and the girls loved him and swooned whenever they saw him. I think his girlfriend was very lucky that he didn't get spirited away by a gaggle of pretty and amorous young ladies who seemed to follow Steve wherever they could! He was very much in demand and spent a lot of time hailing taxis to escape the trial and tribulations of being the good looking lad from the hit children's drama series, *Follyfoot*. Despite these demands on his daily life, I think he secretly loved it!

Originally, I had been given the opportunity to play Steve Ross in *Follyfoot*. Sadly, the director and I had very different views, and after a month's filming it was mutually agreed that I should leave the series. That's when Steve Hodson took over my role. It was a shame as it would have meant that I could have worked with the horses for several months of the year, and still have fitted in a series of *Bless this House*.

People thought that Steve and I were bad enemies when we did the edition of *Whodunnit?* together. Sorry, but that was not true at all. There were no problems at all with him taking over from me in *Follyfoot*. I wasn't right for the part, and he was. My only complaint was that he gave some great parties, and I was never able to get to any of them! At one stage he released a record called 'Crystal Bay', which was written by Maurice Gibb and Billy Lawrie, and went on to appeared in a number of TV series' after *Follyfoot* ended. I believe he now concentrates on acting in audio book and radio play productions.

As mentioned earlier in this book, some of my free time away from *Bless this House* allowed me to indulge myself in my passion for horses. I have been involved with most aspects of the horse world, from show jumping to the point to point, to endurance riding on my beloved Arabians, and finally, of course, the race track. This is where Sid James and I had a good horsey link. We would both give more than one bookie a damn good holiday! Oh, but don't get me wrong, both Sid and I had loyal and very faithful runners that did make up for the horses that didn't exactly romp home as winners! Eventually I gave up punting and took up the gentle art of breeding and riding horses in different countries.

I have been to places on horseback that so few people have ever seen due to their accessibility. Life in the saddle can be amazing if you love beautiful views and challenging climbs, riding to a picnic on a sloping river bank or training for an event that needs you to be as fit as your horse. The spirits of both man and animal being joined together as one is just such an amazing experience and can bring an enormous amount of joy into one's life. That is, of course, if you enjoy that sort of thing. I know others who prefer golf or race cars or just sitting in bars telling tales of conquests and ribald jokes. Still, each to his own.

Although I do love the atmosphere of the race track and the social side like the car park at the Melbourne Cup, I love nothing more than to be alone or with friends out there in the wilderness on a pony. To see their breath in the morning's fresh and stimulatingly cold air is an incredible feeling. It cleanses my soul which is sometimes very necessary.

This reminds me of an occasion on the central coast when I was told that I really should jump my faithful stock horse stallion as well as one of my show jumping mares. Being the idiot that I am, and not wanting to look like a wimp, I gaily walked the novice course and thought to myself that I would give it a go. We started off really well. He lifted his front end and curled up his back legs until half way round were we encountered the very small and, I thought, inviting treble with two strides between each part of the jump. We cleared the first part and as we got to the middle element the brakes came on and I soared through the air and landed on the other side of the poles still holding the reins and, luckily for me, on my feet. To much laughter, and some applause, I walked around the rails, remounted my stead and then jumped a very small, and incredibly easy jump, before leaving the ring. I spent the rest of the day in the beer tent with lots of people slapping me on the back and saying nice things like: 'Nice one, Robin, loved the acrobatics!'

The winner's enclosure at the Melbourne Cup is where I once caught a glimpse of a man wearing a very stylish suit, with a beautiful waist jacket. I thought to myself, I must find out where that chap bought it from. I followed him across the enclosure to ask him, but before I could finish speaking the man turned round and said: 'Hi Robin, How are you?' I took a step back and I realised that it was one of Dr. John Sullivan's boys from New Zealand. John was a legend in not only his profession as a doctor and worldwide lecturer, but he was also as an avid supporter of the trotting industry in New Zealand. One of his real passions was to win the Melbourne Cup because of his love affair with fast horses. And here I was with one of his younger sons (Sean, I think – John and his wife were good Catholics and had many children!) at the Cup wearing, I suddenly realised, one of my suits! No wonder I liked the cut of the suit so much! It was an original Pierre Cardin, too! 'I went over to your farm and borrowed this suit,' he said. 'I had to alter the length of the trousers as they were a bit long!' I think I was too in awe of his cheek to be angry.

Despite all the various acting roles, and other distractions, that came my way during in the first half of the Seventies, it was always nice to return to the bosom of my on screen family in *Bless this House* at Thames TV.

Chapter Six

A Matter Of Privacy

'In those days, the business was so small and vibrant that you only had to sneeze and you ended up in the paper.'

Gary Shail

Although success in the public eye can bring a number of enjoyable rewards, it can lead to a performer losing the privacy he or she once took for granted. Robin reflects in this chapter how becoming well-known changed his life, and how the perception the public had of him varied depending on the roles he played. Robin also goes on to confirm that life became a series of temptations and over indulgence during the times he was away from the Bless this House *team.*

Over the years there have been much said about the subject of fame. Fame is a strange little word that has so many different connotations. What it actually means, none of us really know. Quite a few people have said that it's something that everyone wants, even though they had no idea what it actually entails. Basically it means saying goodbye to any form of private life of any description. And I can say with some authority that if people cannot think of something that is publicly attributed to you, then they will either make it up or try to work out why there is no dirt to dig up!

If you achieve any form of fame, people instantly feel they have the right to discuss your past or present position in life. You can be lost in a crowd of people, with no one taking any notice of you, but it can take only one person to point the finger and say isn't that so and so and then suddenly you're the centre of attention. Before you know it all your moves are being watched and criticised. Are you drinking too much or too little? Is the person that you're talking to straight or gay? Are they a villain or some person of good or bad reputation?

I used to know an actor called Jack Thompson who just happened to live with two young ladies who were sisters. If Jack was seen out and about, nearby conversations would inevitably always start with the words: 'Hey, that's Jack Thompson. Did you know that he lives with two chicks who are sisters?!' The conversation would then usually become what one can only be described as degrading.

I once had had a person in a restaurant in Double Bay in Sydney make a comment about the dirt on my car which I'd parked outside. It happened to be a Range Rover and it was covered in bull dust because I lived in a drought area and we'd been asked to conserve water. I was amazed that it was of such interest. I went outside and wrote on the large back window: 'Drought area car'. A bit later on I heard the following comment coming from the same person at a nearby table: 'I happen to know that he lives in the country, so you would think he could give it a clean in the river'. This is just a tiny example of what takes precedence in some people's minds.

The TV audience is so vast and so kind in its majority that it does, of course, take away a lot of your private life. Because you're on TV in people's living rooms, kitchens and bedrooms, as well as in their newspapers and comic strips, revealing your innermost secrets, they feel they know you. It does also give you an amazing feeling of being needed, wanted and loved. In some cases it can also make you feel hated! This can lead you to having an inflated sense of your own self-importance. So like a tree in a howling wind, you can either stand tall or crash into you own abyss. The choice is, at least, yours, and the outcome is always fascinating because when it comes down to it you only have to answer to yourself. I would advise anyone new to the industry to make the most of it and try to learn from their mistakes. I would also suggest to them they never lose the ability to laugh at themselves because the minute you take it all too seriously you invite a number of problems into your life.

I think that people really do believe that being in an ongoing series is the best thing since sliced bread. Having been in both a long-running sitcom and a soap, I must admit that the sitcom was by far the best type of series to be involved with.

Over the years, I discovered that to some viewers the characters, and the places they inhabit, in soaps are real. The way that script writers used to come up with new ideas for characters in soap operas – especially the villains who both annoy and delight the viewers at the same time – used to fascinate me. That was until I appeared in in two soaps for a period of six months in each, and a third for a slightly shorter time. It was only then that I discovered that the plot lines were practically the same. If you watch a few soaps during the same period, each have very similar characters who all do the same thing over and over again, never failing to keep the viewer totally immersed in their problems. Storylines such as: boy meets girl, boy is actually gay. Girl meets boy, girl is secretly going out with new boy's best friend. Everybody is going out with each other or everybody has gone out with everybody and doesn't want anyone to know! Nobody is left unscathed and all the players are somehow affected, even if they're not related or even involved in the situation.

If you're playing a villain in a soap, then the supermarket can become a battle ground for the unprepared soapy actor! The first accosting is the worst because it is so totally unexpected. The prod in the back, the hit across the back of the head from an irate old lady whose hero you were nasty to last week. Then there's the hard glare from the person who isn't quite sure if it is you or not. But, just in case it is, you get the most hateful look. Woe betide you should confront the adversary head on. The ensuing venom and rudeness can be unbelievable. Often there is no escape and you can find yourself cornered in the frozen food aisle. Without any warning you find yourself paying for what the director and the script writer/s asked you to perform. Meanwhile, the said director and script writer/s is probably blissfully enjoying a gin and tonic somewhere nice and friendly. The viewers don't know or care who they are and are completely oblivious to the fact that you're currently being taken to task for scenes you innocently recorded weeks ago. Although I sometimes wondered if they were secretly jealous and wished they were getting the same attention in the supermarket that I actually wanted to avoid!

Now appearing in a sitcom is a completely different kettle of fish. People pat you on the back instead of hitting you. They make you feel as if you're a long lost friend. That's because you were in their living room only a day or two ago and they were laughing with you at something that Sid, Jean, Sally or I had done or said.

We all know that even back then there were no new jokes. Everything has been said a million times before in sitcom land. Despite this, Sid somehow took the oldest of mannerisms or the most tired of sayings and lines and revitalised them to the degree that we never imagine that it has all been seen before. So when people used to stop me in the street or at the supermarket, they only remembered the things that made them laugh. People would always say in all seriousness: 'Oh, and Mike, you don't mind me calling you Mike, do you?' Then they would generally recollect parts of an episode of *Bless this House* they had watched, and I'd be standing there trying desperately to remember what they were talking about!

Being in a sitcom, where the public love you and the situations that you get put into, is so much more fun than being hated in a soap where all the storylines are all about hardship and suffering. Although I did hear myself voicing the opposite point during a masterclass I took part in at an Australia university. I argued then that getting a reaction of any kind was what was most important!

I read an old *TV Times* magazine interview recently that I took part in we were taping *Bless this House*. It brought back memories me of a nasty experience I once had with a member of the public in the street. Here's an extract from the magazine interview:

> How cross is he (Robin) if his appearance is taken as a sign of homosexuality? "It doesn't worry me what people think, but surely they don't have to make remarks at a person in the street?
>
> "I was accosted not so long ago in Charing Cross Station by a little Scottish chap who said: 'Are you queer or something? 'Are you an old queen? Are you gay? And when I invited him to call a policeman he spat in my face and walked off."

I think that when you find out that you no longer have a private life, it's too late and the damage has been done. Now all that is left to do is to work out how to handle the changes to your life because there are changes and they're very much part of your new life whether you like it or not. The problem for me was that back then nobody told you the rules. No-one gave me lessons on how to cope with being in the public eye.

When I was doing a summer season in Bournemouth one year I used to spend time in the day sitting by the hotel pool. It came to my attention one afternoon that a certain wine waiter seemed to trip up and send a well-known person headlong into the pool. By strange coincidence, there was a guy there with a camera taking shots of the whole event. You might well be wondering how the photographer knew this was going to happen? Or how come he had a camera at just that right time when the supposed accident happened? You'll probably have a few more questions come to mind when I tell you that a day later the photograph in question appeared in an a national newspaper with an appropriate headline. Well, the gentleman who was taking the photos had given the wine waiter a fiver to trip up the unsuspecting personality. This was so he would fall into the pool. The idea was that the photographer took the photographs and sold them to whichever of the national newspapers wanted to buy them. I later found out later that this photographer set up this trick on a regular basis and made between sixty-five and one hundred and twenty pounds per picture. But it all it cost him was just five pounds and the cost of a courier. Sadly, it was the beginning of the new style of paparazzi!

Appearing on TV can result in you being thrust more and more into the public eye, and not always in the best way. It's very difficult to be in the right place at the right time, it's much easier, and of much more value to a journalist, if you can be placed in the wrong place and at the wrong time.

I purposely have not mentioned any personal details in this book that could in any way hurt people during my life with whom I might, or might not, have shared any form of intimacy. It might have sold a few extra books, but is it worth opening up old wounds and destroying someone else's day? I don't think so.

The irony is that I had I not been in the public eye, then nobody would have ever been interested in what I did or didn't do back then. I must admit that there have been times when I have felt so sorry for some of the people who were around me in those heady days. I don't think that the notoriety that one sometimes attracts is everybody's cup of tea. With *Bless this House* achieving so much success, our notoriety was tenfold and for this little actor it all became obvious very quickly that I had not escaped the notoriety that so many craved. I had no idea what was lurking just around the corner waiting to bite me. Being Mike Abbott was not always the best person to be, especially when the PR machine was at work!

Looking back, I recall that there were a few rather misleading headlines printed in various publications. 'How Robin Stewart Got High' was a bit of a worry, especially as the actual article was on hang gliding, a favourite sport at the time. I think one of the best misleading headlines I read was printed in New Zealand. The headline stated: 'Get Out Shock For Robin Stewart' before proceeding to talk about another entertainer who had been asked to leave the country. The only connection that it had on me was a line that said: 'What if this happens to Robin?' This line was only written because the acting union over there thought that a New Zealander should have the job of hosting *Opportunity Knocks* instead of me. They conveniently forget that the government had given me residency. If I hadn't been in a hit series, then no one would have cared. Yes, I think that one can safely say I have had my fair share of mediocre publicity. I am afraid that if you put yourself up there to be counted, you just have to grin and bear it.

Oscar Wilde once said: 'I can resist everything except temptation'. And that's certainly true of me! I found that if I stayed in town for too long I inevitably got carried away with whatever was going on at the time. Admittedly, there was a time when I forgot who I really was. I'm certainly not the only person in the world that has experienced that feeling. I think that it's a sort of whirlwind effect when one just gets carried along by the moment until the moment becomes the all important thing in one's life. It's a snowball effect, and once it starts to roll, well, the old saying is so correct: 'A rolling stone gathers no moss'. One ends up going from one club to another, one party to another and one pub to another. Pubs were an incredible link to both reality and fantasy in those days because they were not just a place to meet mates or have a drink, they were a stepping stone to anywhere you wanted to be at the time.

If was sitting and reading a newspaper in one pub or another people would often pat me on the back as they came past and would say things like: 'Hey Robsie, catch you in the back bar,' or 'When you've finished reading, come and have a cocktail'. It was then I either continued to read or slowly folded up the paper and joined whoever it was that had just made contact. It didn't really matter because eventually they would come back and then the whole game would began. A quick nod at the bar staff, who were always ready to serve, and the chat would start. Then within no time at all there would be a small gathering of employed and unemployed actors. The group invariably got joined by an eclectic mix of other individuals, such as car dealers and fantasists who believed their own lies.

We were all a bit foolish back then. There was lots of laughter, too much liquid and not enough to occupy one's time to present the inevitable partying. Life was just a merry-go-round of working or not working. Real time meant absolutely nothing if you weren't on call for an acting job few days. And if I was in town the temptation to eat, drink and talk about everything and nothing all at the same time was very strong. Yes, some of us might have been well-known thespians who were working in TV, making a film or doing voice overs, but not at that very moment. No, right then we were successful reprobates let off the leash and having, what we thought, was a great time. Someone would say something like: 'Hey, I am off to Gerry's Bar. Anyone coming?' Gerry's Bar was an actor's drinking club in Shaftesbury Avenue, and both Gerry's and The Green Room were both safe places for an actor to hide. Then we'd end up visiting more bars and fashionable night clubs of the time. The last port of call was Ronnie Scott's, and, if that wasn't enough, we'd then take breakfast at the old Barclay Hotel. This was long before it moved from Piccadilly to Knightsbridge. I probably shouldn't mention this, but back in those days, if you had any sort of fame, you could have a little whiskey put into your tea pot instead of the usual tea leaves. It went down well with kippers and toast, if you had a strong constitution!

My good mate, the actor Gary Shail, also has an interesting take on my socialising at the time:

> Having started in the business ten years after Robin, my mates and I were well aware of everybody who

was a working actor and who was just out there. Peter O'Toole, Jimmy Villiers, Ronnie Fraser, Patrick Wymark, Paddy Newell, Richard Harris, with or without his chauffeur come minder, Reg Lock, and a host of others were a little crew who were sometimes branded as "bad boys and girls". In those days, the business was so small and vibrant that you only had to sneeze and you ended up in the paper. And believe me, I had it all in front of me when I went on to appear in *Quadrophenia* and *Metal Micky*.

Before *Bless this House*, Rob could get away with murder. People knew his face, and they thought they knew him, but they couldn't work out where from. After *Bless this House* came out that "long haired layabout" could not move without someone shouting "Oi! How's Sid?" Or "I don't half fancy you sister!" The dye was cast and Robin lost his private life.

He used to be seen at the Crazy E in Jermyn Street, later to become Dolly's, the Ad Lib Nightclub off Leicester Square, and the Scotch of St. James. After Dante and Mino took over the Speak Easy, there was Robin. The Playboy had a disco run by Tony Doyle, and Robin was either there or gambling with Telly Savalas in the gaming area. Failing that, he could be found at The Victoria Sporting Club in the Edgware Road. Wherever the action was, you would find him. We all thought it was great – well that was until some of us achieved the same notoriety! We soon realised that it wasn't easy to have a great time and not be noticed doing it. And boy, did we all learn quickly that being in the public eye is not all gin and roses.

In the good old days, pop groups could go to the clubs to join actors like Robin, David Hemmings and Steve Marriot. We loved them and followed them ten years later. What a buzz! We are all just calm now, although what we all got up to was so tame compared to the likes of Justin Bieber these days!

It was all tame and harmless fun, and the only damage we did was to ourselves! For instance, in The Sir Richard Steele Pub in Belseize Park, north London, you would sometimes find Paddy Newell, who played 'Mother' in the action TV series, *The Avengers*. During a stay in hospital, a doctor once told Patrick that if he had one more drink he would die. This caused the actor to give up drinking immediately, and lose a great deal of weight in the process. Ironically, poor Paddy didn't work for ages after this because the TV companies did not want a 'thin' Paddy Newel. It can be a very cruel business at times.

The late Patrick Wymark, who appeared in a popular TV series in the Sixties called *The Power Game,* was basically told the same thing as Paddy. Patrick tried very hard to stop drinking, but when we were doing *Cromwell* his Bloody Mary's looked more and more anaemic every day. Unfortunately, that meant only one thing: the tomato juice in the Bloody Mary was, once again, being taken over by the vodka.

As I mentioned, if I stayed in town, things could get wild. Then again, my memories of my country life in Australia include long after-hour drinking sessions in my local country pub, and then riding a horse home through the paddock. On many an occasion there would be a few people getting a lift home in the early morning mist through fields watched by semi-interested cows. Heaven knows what they thought! Great times! My personal experience is that it was a lot safer spending my days off in the bush. In town there were far too many people intent on ruining your day. In the country it's all so much more relaxed. And getting into trouble usually just means a dose of good old-fashioned mischief!

Chapter Seven

Life After Bless This House

'You know, Robin, you should skip.'

Sid James

Negotiations were in the process of taking place for a possible seventh series while the sixth series of Bless this House *was broadcast in 1976. But, as you will discover in this chapter, Robin's life and career were both to take a different direction after the sudden and untimely death of Sid James in the April of that year. After recalling his days touring in a play called* The Murder Game, *Robin goes on to describe how he felt after Sid passed away, and the abiding memories he has of his onscreen father. The remainder of the chapter includes Robin taking us back to the days he hosted the New Zealand version of the talent show,* Opportunity Knocks, *his experiences of appearing on Australian daytime soap operas, and touring in the John Godber play,* Up 'n' Under.

The Murder Game was a play that I did in the UK during a break between series' of *Bless this House*. It was a strange play by Constance Cox, and the main players were John Bentley and myself. John, was born in Melbourne in Australia, and was loved the fact that he was remembered by all the older ladies in the audience. The only problem was that he was not at all happy about the fact that they remembered him as a younger, good looking man, and he got very depressed about his age. But he was lovely to work with, even though he simply couldn't adjust to growing old gracefully.

John's knowledge of Hollywood, and producing films like *Istanbul* with Errol Flynn, and working closely with the likes of Vera Miles and Barbara Stanwyck, gave way to many a long and interesting discussion into the night. And, of course, who could forget that memorable series that Bentley did in Africa called *African Patrol*. It was sold worldwide and achieved unbelievably high ratings in the USA. I'm sure there are many of you reading this book that will remember him playing Hugh Mortimer, Meg Richardson's ill-fated husband in the ATV soap opera, *Crossroads*.

John's character in the play supposedly ran into me with his car and took pity on me. He then let me move into his house to give me time to recover. During the first half of the play my character changes from being a well-adjusted young man to a complete and utter psychopath. He ends up doing one of the fastest costume changes on stage, without the audience realising at first. He's suddenly right there, back on the sofa, wearing a blonde grey wig and suitably attired as a woman. He then blackmails the character that John played, strangling his lover and takes over the house. It really was a very dark play.

During the run of the show we had to vacate the theatre that we were appearing at because the bomb squad had to be called in. They found an item stashed away in an air conditioning unit in the back of my dressing room. I don't think it was specifically planted there to hurt me. After about forty-five minutes waiting outside, we went back into the theatre and continued with the play. Not an easy task I can tell you!

It was while I was appearing in *The Murder Game* that I received a phone call in the early hours of the morning from a reporter who told me that Sid James had died. Without pausing for breath, he asked me for a comment. I thought it was a crank call at first. Then, an hour or so later started to receive more phone calls. That was when I realised that the news was for real. I can remember having to sit down. I felt completely numb. It didn't seem possible that he could have died. He was invincible, he was, well, Sid! I thought of his wife, Val, and their children, Steve and Susan. Then, of course, I thought of Diana and Sally.

The next few days were a bit of a blur and I don't think that reality actually took a hold for about a week. People said things like: 'What's going to happen now to *Bless this House*?' It was so strange because that never seemed to come into the equation. Sid James and work were never in the same sentence. Sid was my Dad on the telly, not someone that I worked with. The cast were like the family I lived with at Thames TV.

It was an awful time and my heart went out to his real family, and I personally felt very alone. It was a very strange feeling and I find it hard to describe. It was as if a huge gap had opened up in my life and there was no way of filling it. I couldn't actually explain it.

For Diana, Sally and I the feelings were all so diverse. I know that I personally felt a great loss. We may have only been together for a short time each year, but during that time we, as a cast, were all very close. I think it's fair to say that we were all a bit devastated and a lost for a while. The expression 'gone but not forgotten' certain applies to Sid. He has never been forgotten and I am always asked the same question everywhere I go: 'What was it like working with Sid, Robin?'

My only disappointment in all the years that I knew Sid was that I never once managed to be able to watch him perform live on stage. I would have loved to have sat in the audience and just laughed at the man who played my Dad and felt proud.

I was asked earlier this year if there was one piece of advice that Sid gave me that has stayed with me. The answer is yes – there is. We were in the middle of rehearsals for an episode of *Bless this House* one day when I suddenly became aware that Sid was looking at me. He must have seen me looking back because he beckoned me over to him. Wondering what I had done wrong, I made my way over to him somewhat sheepishly.

'You know, Robin,' he said casually. 'You should skip.'

'Sorry?' I said somewhat taken aback.

'Skip,' he said. 'Because when everything gives up, you can always stand at a microphone and read lines.'

He had a point.

'If your legs are strong you can keep working,' he continued. 'And you can always get to and from the car!'

Sid winked and I took that as a hint that you can always get yourself to the bookies! I laughed.

'I am being serious,' Sid said.

Speaking of the bookies reminds me that Sid and I once did a Super Yankee Bet that had a particularly good result! I picked the winnings up the following Tuesday from Twickenham. I will not disclose the amount, but let's just say that pockets bulged with a vulgarity that I wish could happen all the time! Horses that should never have even left home romped across the finish line as if they were bred to win! It was just a very lucky weekend. I think William G. Stewart also put the odd bet on for Sid too. I just did as I was told and sometimes reaped the benefits. There were, of course, those horses that lost us both a few quid, but we don't talk about them! Both Sid and I had the odd trainer and jockey who, for a small fee, would give us the odd horse that might just win or get a good place. Life was so much fun in those days. We were all so lucky to have known Sid, or at least the man he was willing to let us know.

After Sid passed away I was asked to go to New Zealand with the comedian and actor Michael Bentine, and *Love Thy Neighbour*'s Nina Baden-Semper, to appear on their telethon. This was staged in aid of Muscular Dystrophy in children. It was an admirable appeal and a pleasure to help them. I took a leave of absence from *The Murder Game*, and was back within a week. And that included the travel times there and back. It was a hectic schedule and I remember having very little sleep.

I did a cameo in the 1977 saucy comedy film, *Adventures of a Private Eye*. It was a lot of fun and my old mates Diana Dors and Harry H. Corbett starred in the production.

The film featured the assistant of a private detective whose attempts to solve a case lead to a number of problems. My cameo role, for want of a better expression, saw me playing a photographer called Scott. It called for me to end up in bed with a lot of mouse traps. I was filmed jumping about like a man who obviously had a lot of lot of traps firmly attached to his private bits! It was a far cry from the family friendly storylines I was used to in *Bless this House*!

Diana Dors was not someone that I had worked with until I appeared in this film. She was a joy to be with both on and off set. I remember her house just outside Windsor where many people came and joined both her and Leepy Lee for a libation and a snack. In those days, when the TV channels closed around midnight, Diana and her guests, including myself, used to play a game which was called, amongst other things, 'The Religious Moment'. This was due to there being a closing programme – called *The Epilogue* – at the time which was presented by a religious person of some denomination or other. We always wondered why there was nothing ever on for the agnostic or the atheist. Anyway, the idea was that the sound was turned off and then you asked a question before the sound was quickly turned back on. I cannot reveal what the questions were. What I will say is that they were not in keeping with the programme context or content! But with the sound now on full blast the unsuspecting person talking gave the answer to the question with some hilarious results! *The Epilogue* was never quite the same again after you'd played this game. Rest in peace, Diana, and thank you for all the laughs!

The reaction from my first appearance in New Zealand on their telethon was very gratifying, and, after much negotiation, I moved to the country so I could host their version of *Opportunity Knocks*.

Opportunity Knocks was originally hosted in the UK by Hughie Green, and in Australia by Johnny Farnham. Having never ever presented a show on my own, apart from a radio programme in America when I was fourteen, hosting the New Zealand version was, to say the least, very daunting.

The producer of the series was Tom Parkinson, who I had worked with on *H.M.S. Defiant*, but not that closely. Parkinson was from England and was a resident in New Zealand with an amazing background in all forms of entertainment. He was an incredible force. I remember the first production meeting when he was asked by the sound man, who, I have to admit was not the greatest of allies, where my script was. He replied that he didn't have a copy and neither did the camera crew. Tom's answer was simple: 'Just make sure you stay on Robin. I will call the shots from the OB van and Robin, being an old tart at this game, will be exactly where I want him to be. Now if there are no more questions I think it's time for lunch'.

Pleasingly, the show's ratings were far higher than anyone could have predicted. This saw Equity, the actors' union, awarded a foot-in-the-mouth award via a cartoon in a New Zealand newspaper for not supporting my engagement on the show from the very beginning. Eventually I became a committee member of the subsidiary variety club committee.

I went live to air on the finals of the show on both years, with special guests including a member of The Beach Boys. One of the winner's prizes was to perform live on *The Mike Walsh Show* in Australia.

Between the end of the first and the start of the second series of *Opportunity Knocks*, I was asked to host *Miss New Zealand*. Now this show had the reputation of being the highest rating show on TV2. This is arguably due to lots of attractive girls appearing on the show in bikinis! The crew were all the same as my *Opportunity Knocks* crew so I felt very comfortable.

During the live broadcast, Murray, who was my floor manager, suddenly appeared under the crane camera to inform me that I only had fifteen seconds to go to the commercial break. Knowing I had to be quick, I said: 'Well, ladies and gentlemen, I'm delighted that I'm not a judge because let's face it the longer you look, the harder it gets!' We then went straight to the break. No problem – or so I thought! Cut to the next day when, having landed back in Auckland, I strolled back to the TV2 head office. Everywhere I looked at the studio people were pointing at me and laughing. They kept saying: ...the longer you look, the harder it gets!' They were also making comments like: 'Good on you, Robs,' while smiling like Cheshire cats. I went to one of the editing suites to look at the footage of the previous night's live show. It never occurred to me that my innocent line would be taken quite so literally! It was just a quick innocent line off the top of my head. I certainly didn't mean for it to cause any offence. Anyway, to cut a long story the newspaper in Dunedin decided I was crude and rude and not welcome in their fair city! How times have changed.

I also became a permanent member of the panel on their version of *Celebrity Squares* while I was in New Zealand. At the same time I was being seen each week in repeats of *Bless this House*, and making guest appearances in a variety show with singers and dancers there called *Top of the World*. I couldn't, and still can't, sing or dance, but they somehow managed to fit me in to the show.

TV appearances also came courtesy of the *Hudson and Halls* chat show. It was a bit like *Alan Carr's Chatty Man* in the UK, although they combined their chat show with a cooking segment. The audiences loved it. In some ways it was before its time. They also came over here to the UK and stayed with Anita Harris and Mike Margolis for a while, I think. But the duo didn't achieve the same success as they did on their home turf. Sadly, Peter and David were parted from each other, both personally and professionally, when Hudson died of cancer in 1992. Tragically, Halls took his own life in 1993.

I think that by the end of each week all the TV2 viewers in New Zealand must have been pretty fed up with my face! The viewing audience was not that big as at that time, I think there were only about three million people, maybe less. I forget as it was a while ago now. There were only two channels in total at the time: TV1 and TV2, both of which, if I am not mistaken, were owned by the New Zealand broadcasting corporation. You could say that they had a bit of a monopoly. Anyway, I wouldn't have missed it for the world!

When I accepted the invitation to go and work in New Zealand, I had no idea that I would be away from the UK for so long. I thought I would be away for maybe a year or eighteen months at the most. Then the actor Derek Nimmo invited me over to Australia for the Melbourne Cup, and everything changed again. I ended up being signed to Bedford & Pearce Management, a company run by Martin Bedford and Shirley Pearce. They handled most of the many of the soap stars of that period.

I was then invited to go to Australia where I became a guest on *The Peter Couchman Show*. Then it was off to Bunbury WA to do another telethon, before going back to Sydney to be a guest on *The Mike Walsh Show*. A couple of weeks were later spent co-hosting *Good Morning Sydney* with Maureen Duval. Working on the show allowed me the enviable opportunity to eat at some fantastic restaurants because one of my enjoyable tasks was to review them for the show.

I will never forget the morning that I arrived at the *Good Morning Sydney* studio and was introduced a power-dressed young lady who was a spokesperson for the RSPCA. I noticed that the crew were all secretly giggling like a pack of hyenas. When I asked them what they were laughing at, they told me to wait and see. It wasn't long before I discovered the reason. The power-dressed young lady came on to the set and all I remember about the following interview is that I said 'hello' and 'goodbye'. I couldn't get a single word in edgeways, and I don't think she paused to take even a single breath! The expression 'lost for words' could never be a comment that could be attributed to her!

I had a much better time chatting with actor Mel Gibson on another edition of the show. This was mainly due to the fact that when he was at NIDA (National Institute of Dramatic Art) he often came over to my place in Sydney chilling before the night's revelry took over. We had a great time laughing and both talked about the same amount as my RSPCA friend, but without any power dressing being involved!

In 1981, I spent six months appearing in the hospital-based soap, *The Young Doctors*. In case you're too young to remember this series, which was also shown in the UK, it featured the romantic goings between the staff at the Albert Memorial Hospital in Sydney. When the staff weren't attempting to hide their lustful thoughts in the wards and the operating theatres, they were acting upon them in a local bar called Bunny's.

The series, created by Alan Coleman (who was once quotes as saying 'We're making the show for the viewers, not the critics'), was my very first experience of appearing in a high-rating, fast turnaround daytime TV soap. The cast and crew worked incredibly hard and the words 'take two' were hardly ever heard. It was a real eye opener. The cast, which at one time included Alan Dale best-known for his appearances in *Neighbours* and *Ugly Betty*, worked for very little money. If their agents asked for more dosh, then their characters suddenly became surplus to requirement.

I did my mandatory six months in *The Young Doctors* and the moved on to play the role of Hopgood in another soap called *Punishment*. My character was a verbal muscleman. He used to threatens people in various ways but then send the boys round to do the actual dirty work! Hopgood was a good character to play, though. There are lots of things you can do with that sort of character. He was not a one-dimensional, cardboard figure. It was just a pity that my stint only lasted for four weeks.

Continuing the soap theme, three years later I went on to do a stint in *Sons and Daughters* playing a doctor called Ross Newman.

The series, which was created by Reg Watson and produced by the Reg Grundy Organisation, ran between 1982 and 1987. It charted, to quote the theme song, the 'love and laughter, tears and sadness and happiness' of the Palmer, Hamilton, Morrell and O'Brien families and the friends and families.

Despite the series being taped in Sydney, the storylines was set in both Melbourne as well as Sydney. This meant that members of the cast and crew used fly to Melbourne from time-to-time to shoot scenes there.

Sons and Daughters won the 'Logie Award for Most Popular Australian Drama' in 1983, and a number of cast members, including Rowena Wallace, won awards throughout the various seasons.

Admittedly, UK audiences tend to remember the soap for two main reasons. Firstly, the catchy theme tune, which was written by Peter Pinne & Don Battye, and performed by Mick Leyton and Kerri Biddell. Secondly, they remember the end credits rolling over a freeze-frame sepia shot of one of the characters striking a particularly dramatic pose. I'm told comedians used to send-up the latter in their acts and series back in the days when it used to be shown on the ITV network.

My character was a gambling-obsessed surgeon who ended up with serious gambling debts. One of my biggest storylines involved me nearly knocking down the character of Patricia Morrell (a major character). If you thought that was bad enough, she was fleeing a gunman at the time! But worse was to come. After further bizarre twists and turns in the story, my character conceived a plan to kill her on the operating table. Let's just say my storylines were in the best tradition of Aussie soaps!

In the late Seventies and throughout the Eighties every aspiring young actor in Australia wanted to be recognised and the Aussie soaps were the only real way to get that kind of following. They seemed to live their characters both on and off screen. The younger players had a hard time of it because their fees did not really allow them to keep up with the lifestyle they thought they should be living. The older players had a much better time of it, financially speaking, and we managed to enjoy the lifestyle that we wanted. I know that my horses ate well and there was always red wine on the table.

While I was appearing in *Sons and Daughters*, the powers that be in the real world decided that the mining companies of Australia needed yet another open cut mine. This was to add to their already overloaded mining ventures in the Hunter Valley. It was located in one of the beauty spots and famous wine-producing areas of the Hunter region. The mainstay of the cast came with me to demonstrate against the governments decisions to destroy yet another lush and serene area of Australia in the name of profit.

I got to know many actors who had great success in Australia, especially in soapland. They include Tom Oliver (Lou Carpenter in *Neighbours*), Ian Smith (Harold Bishop in *Neighbours*) and Ray Meagher (Alf Stewart in *Home and Away*). Ray and I both did a commercial for Cup-a-Soup together in Tasmania and never stopped laughing. We even managed to have fun galloping along the beach, despite the sea almost engulfing our regal steads up to their necks in salt water.

I brought a dinner jacket on the trip so I could look the part at the local casino. Ray thought this was a completely insane thing to do – he was right! Apart from the wine waiters, I was the only one in a tux. I was continually being asked to get drink orders for people. Amusing to some, but not me as I was intent on some serious card playing. In the end I gave up and we went out for dinner instead. The problem was I felt even more over-dressed!

When we arrived at Hobart, Ray was keen to induct me in their serving protocol at the first bar we visited.

'Robin keep your hand up in the air,' he explained.

'Why?' I asked.

'Mate,' he replied. 'This is Tassie. If your hand isn't up you won't get another drink. Over here there is no rush and if you look as if you're relaxed, even if your glass is empty, the staff will leave you alone!'

In the end my arm could have done with a splint as it stayed up for so long!

Now when I watch Ray playing Alf Stewart in *Home and Away* I smile as I reflect on the great times we spent together.

I also knew and worked with Ray Barrett and Bill Kerr. Both actors enjoyed tremendous success in the UK for before going back home to Australia.

I appeared in a series about the oil industry many years ago with Ray called *The Trouble Shooters*. This propelled him into immediate stardom both on screen and on the golf course! Ray was always a pleasure to be around and a great mate to share a drink with. I worked with him again in Australia on the ABC mini-series, *Timeless Land*, in the early Eighties. It was the same series in which had to take part in a dueling scene with another actor. During the filming we were suddenly alerted to the fact that there were two Aboriginal men paddling against the current on the river behind us. I never actually found out for definite if they were working for the production or not. I have a feeling that they were told to keep paddling while we were shooting the scene. It soon became quite clear as they paddled vigorously that their small craft was taking on water. In due course they slowly started to sink and disappear from view. They never stopped paddling until there was nothing left to see except for their heads. Only then did they choose to abandon their craft and slowly started to breaststroke their way towards the shore. With a degree of admirable nonchalance, they did this as if nothing untoward had happened!

I personally suffered a bit of a dental disaster during the filming of *Timeless Land*. I had to mount my trusty steed and look very important while outside the Blyth House set. I realised that the guy who was holding my horse had not been told that I was used to handling and riding horses. He hung on to the now very agitated horse in such a way that I had no control of it at all. As my right leg lifted over the horse's rump, my sword gently caressed his already twitchy top line. The horse then decided to buck on the spot. My leg was only half way across his behind and the handler, for his own safety, I imagine, suddenly let go and the horse left our mark and galloped across the nearby fields. I found myself in that rather embarrassing position of being dumped onto the ground. Unfortunately this was not before the stirrup iron had firmly and quite painfully whacked into my face. This later caused me to lose two front teeth. Sadly, none of us get out of this movie industry unscathed, and it's not just the press that cause the damage! Horses for courses, and, as I'm sure you can imagine it wasn't just my pride that was hurt that day!

Going back a little, what can one say about Bill Kerr? Bill left Australia to become an integral part of the Tony Hancock's radio series, *Hancock's Half Hour*, with Sid James. When he returned to his beloved Australia he was welcomed with open arms. He spent time with me in Yarramalong Valley mostly sitting on the steps of the veranda talking to a then young model Elle Macpherson. I then did the same with Bill in Perth, a town that he loves so much.

Back in the late Seventies I got involved with a paddle boat business and doing radio and TV in Townsville. I was taking on clients and writing and producing their commercials for radio and TV. It was while I was in Townsville that I met Tony Gordon, who had just moved on from being a senior cameraman to head his own production company. This is something he still does when he's not filming documentaries. I was privileged to be at his wedding many years ago and the whole family have remained great and staunch friends ever since. I was really blown away with the following piece he sent me for inclusion within this book:

> Tony: A bloke called Bluey Vaughan, who lives in the North West Kimberley's, once said to me: "There are people who bring you pleasure when they arrive and there are those who bring you pleasure when they go". Meeting Robin Stewart was the former, and it's sad that he has left Australia and returned back to England. However, this is very understandable considering his long and vibrant career on stage and screen in the UK.

My association and friendship with Robin has seen us both through a raft of stages in life, commencing when he was writing, producing and directing TV advertising for Channel 10 in Townsville in the Seventies, to his much loved horse breeding days in recent times.

We can learn a lot from people who come into our lives and sometimes what you learn sticks with you, and you carry it with you always. A few things Robin has imparted to me over the years have stuck with me always as a constant reminder "not to take one's self too seriously". His demeanour in your presence would always bring with it levity, wit and charm. I have Robin to thank for my appreciation of fine coffee, good wine and women! He has given me skills that hold myself and my children is good stead in times of strife and desperation. His quick wit and command of the language would ensure that he was in charge of any situation – no matter how dire the circumstances might seem. And we often emulate his techniques for dealing with troublesome situations.

While Robin has had a more colourful and varied association with the fairer sex, he has at the same time always had a propensity to bring about his own demise where women are concerned. This is largely due to his unforgiving lack of tolerance when they failed to meet his standards, or keep pace with his 'mile-a-minute' thought process. He is a Bloke's Bloke. His love of the country life and his abilities with animals drew him away from 'the business' and into a life on the land as the 'squire'. A title befitting, no matter where the parcel of land, or what livestock it carried, Robin would always be at home in the countryside, or astride one of his prized Arab stallions.

His entrepreneurial skills are as colourful as the rise and fall of Dow Jones Index. His fortunes came and went in much the same style as the punters who often risked all on a venture only to be piped at the post. One such initiative I recall was his Hot Air Balloon investment, whereby he had come across a 'Blimp' that he intended to sign write and sell advertising at sports events. I do recall seeing said balloon gathering dust under his abode years later without any evidence of having returned its initial purchase price. A similar venture would have been the telescope he purchased from the Picnic Bay Wharf on Magnetic Island, which he had me retrieve for him after it languished in the salt air for a decade.

A visit with Robin would always be a delight no matter where he was, and no matter what circumstances you would encounter him in. He tended to move about not able to settle in one place for long and I attribute this to his heritage of which he has always been extremely proud.

Many people consider Robin as a close valued friend and a delightful person who will entertain and enchant. I like to think that I am among those who have had the privilege of knowing him at depth and with a passion that has and still endures to this moment.

Tony was with me when I decided to bring jazz to Townsville by hiring one of the old-style Hayles ferries. I added a dance floor and took people out to Maggie Island before mooring up at the back of West End to listen to great music each Sunday afternoon. Then, in conjunction with two mates who owned both The Black River Cattle Company and Tony's Seafood, the happy revellers made their way to the latter to eat as many oysters, bugs and prawns as they could possibly stomach!

Just for fun, I would occasionally DJ at the sports and recreation club in Horseshoe Bay. It was, at the time at least, the only nightclub on the island. Friday nights were a locals and back-packer haven. I was also quite heavily involved it the toad races which became quite an interesting income enhancer! The tourists bet on their ability to jump to the edge of a well-defined circle. It was a great night for all!

Another Townsville memory I have revolves around a cyclone! I sat in a friend's place on the esplanade behind double-glazed, reinforced windows while all hell was going on outside. I watched the palm trees leaning over on their sides as the winds blew stronger and stronger. Our radio gave us updated warnings every ten minutes about the impending doom. The apartment was owned by an entrepreneur called Kevin O'Neil who bought over international acts to Australia such as Cliff Richard. Both he and his girlfriend sat there laughing at me as I said things like: 'Ah well, I suppose it's not actually over until the glass breaks and the fat lady sings'. The radio announcer kept giving us safety tips like putting a mattress in front of the windows and adding lots of sticky tape to stop the glass from shattering everywhere. It was like something out of the war! They also suggested that we sheltered in the bath as it was usually in a concrete based room, probably the only one in the house, and just wait for the storm to finish.

After consuming many cocktails, and having a short snooze, the wind stopped and the sea cleared. The sun came out and Magnetic Island reappeared. We turned Bob Marley off and tuned back into the radio station to discover that the cyclone had turned away at the last minute and decided to cause havoc at a town further down the coast.

The year 1981 saw me take to the cinema screen again. This time I played the role of a womaniser called Paul in a comedy called *Pacific Banana.*

Directed by John D. Lamond, *Pacific Banana* featured a couple of pilots and a wind sock that just wouldn't stay up! Basically, it featured Graeme Blundell and myself roving around the Pacific Islands in a DC-3 frolicking with as many woman as we good. Farcical? Yes! Ridiculous? Most certainly! Graeme and I managed to complete the whole picture without revealing any of our 'naughty bits'! We were very proud of that, I can tell you, much to the chagrin of the director. *Pacific Banana* became a bit of a cult film with the footy brigade in Australia, and was dragged out from the video and DVD shops and viewed with a few cans of beer after the game on Saturdays. Fame at last!

Burbank Films, who took the cartoons that I lent my vocal talents to in the early Eighties of the complete works of Charles Dickens and Sir Arthur Conan Doyle, resold them back to Australia. This was ironic as that's where they were made in the first place! I have them all on DVD and my grandchildren were fascinated when they saw them for the first time. However, they have no idea that the faithful carriage driver or handsome swan or Lord Baskerville's brother etc. is their grandfather, and would never believe me if I told them! The younger members of my family never accept that it's me in shows such as *Bless this House*. They just think that's it's someone younger who looks me!

Working on cartoons can be great fun. You quite often you can end up talking to yourself with different voices, and maybe even as an angry growling dog to boot. I did once suffer at the hands of a fun loving, fractionally bored actor during one recording session, though. He decided that it would be ever so funny to set fire to my script while I was talking! It wasn't until I became aware that there were red and yellow plumes of a mini fire erupting from the top off my pages that I realised something was wrong. This was followed by the inevitable crumpling as the fire stated to eat the paper. There was a great deal of laughter around me, but not from the control room. Innocent I might have been, but the small inferno was blamed on me and I was told to 'please stop mucking about!'

I had great fun appearing in another series for children called *Runaway Island: The Treasure of the Conquistadors*. It had a successful run on Channel 7 for the Grundy Organisation in 1985. The cast included Sancho Gracia, a Spanish heart throb and a very hard working actor who sadly died in 2012.

Gracia played Pinero, a typical Spanish hero character, and was loved by the whole cast and crew. I played Pinero's close friend and companion who had been engaged by the King of Spain to paint and immortalise all of their various exploits on canvas. And paint I did, even in the face of the dreaded plague that claimed so many in old Sydney town. In the series, Pinero battled his way through the townships of Sydney after our journey by boat to Australia's far of shores to help an old friend and his children regain their heritage.

It was all great fun and we filmed there for about six weeks at a famous old ranch north of Sydney, which Grundy had cleverly turned into an old-fashioned Australian town.

I then went straight from that into ABC's *Sweet and Sour*, a drama series all about the birth of an Aussie rock band. I played the rather out of kilter manager who did not really help their cause at all. It was a very successful series and we enjoyed good ratings when it was transmitted.

The idea of acting on stage continued to appeal to me. This is probably why I decide to tour Australia in the John Godber play, *Up 'n' Under*. Our director was Richard Lewis, who came over to Australia to direct us. Richard was actually in the film *A Clockwork Orange* and went on to play Phil Hopley in the original production of *Up 'n' Under*. He has also been responsible for stage productions of *Jesus Christ Superstar*, *The Maintenance Man* and *Stepping Out*. So you can imagine how unbelievably fortunate we all felt were to have him as our director. He was a very hard task master, but he did a brilliant job and was one of the most caring directors one could ever hope to work for in the theatre.

I have to admit that playing Arthur Hoyle in *Up 'n' Under* was the most physically demanding acting role that I have ever undertaken. We took part in various sessions in the gym to training to for the rugby game scenes on stage with real weights. Our cross country training runs were done on stage in slow motion to the well-known music from the film *Chariots of Fire*. Breathing in an exaggerated way while running on the spot in very slow motion caused an enormous amount of hyper-ventilation. It was a great strain on all of us. Fortunately, for the other cast members, they all looked like footballers in their gear, and were very 'spunky', as the Australians would say.

We toured this play across Australia for about ten weeks before going into Kinselas in Sydney's heartland. It might have been less, but it certainly felt like a lot more! We kept the chiropractors in holiday money at each venue that we played. The tackling and slow motion lifting was unbelievably strenuous and took its toll on us all.

We had a week off in the middle of the pre-Sydney tour and that's where my love affair with Magnetic Island first began. I was given a motor boat and told to head out seven miles and traverse around the back of the island until I came to Horse Shoe Bay. I was told I couldn't miss it. Typically, the trusty wee speed boat started to splutter well over half-way. Being the impatient intrepid traveler that I am, I kept heading away from the mainland and off around the island. The boat could not have gone any slower, or with more spluttering, and when I eventually got to the jetty at Horse Shoe Bay, which I didn't think I would achieve.

An actor called Jeff, who was also in the play, was standing on the foreshore with a very enterprising young lady. They both thought my problems with the boat were highly amusing!

Once I came to terms with the fact that my feet were at last on terra firma, we headed for, at that time, the only local source of food and drink. And that is where I met the Brackmanski family, who became great mates, for the first time.

When the play had finished its run in Sydney, I went back to spend a much-needed break with the Brackmanski's. George and his lovely wife and I became inseparable, and their children just accepted me as part of the family. We used to go over to the mainland at least twice a week to the casino where we gambled, and had lunch or dinner. I had an agreement with the gambling establishment that if I played there we got fed and really looked after! Then we either stayed over or travelled back on a water taxi.

Looking back, I have to say that this period proved to be one of the most relaxing times of my life. Then I got bored of sitting at the end of the large horseshoe shaped beach. That's when I decided to make my life busy and stressful again!

Chapter Eight

The Eternal Optimist

'It's really down to you to be pleasant anyway, you know, and have a smile on your face, and be nice to people, which isn't difficult.'

Ronnie Corbett

In the final chapter of his book, Robin recalls interviewing Ronnie Corbett in Australia, reaching fifty years-old, indulging the hippie side to his nature, and explaining why the show had to go on even when he was suffering a bereavement. Robin also reveals how his health has paid for living and enjoying life to the extreme. We also learn how the repeats and DVD releases of Bless this House *have led to Robin and his former screen sister, Sally Geeson, being reunited for appearances at conventions and special events.*

During one point in the Nineties I hosted and produced a show for DDQ TV in Australia called *Midweek Live*. This saw me interviewing various overseas guests. One of my celebrity guests was the legendary comedian and actor, Ronnie Corbett.

Meeting and interviewing Ronnie was a real highlight for me. He was, and remains, a great raconteur and a joy to be with. We spent about ninety-minutes together laughing, grinning and generally just having fun during the making of *Ronnie Corbett: Man of Laughter*. My camera crew could not believe the camaraderie we had, and the overall atmosphere that was created. We traded lines and talked about favourite foods, his, not mine, and places to holiday and people of a grumpy nature on the golf course. We, of course, also spoke at length about Ronnie Barker and his brilliance. He also regaled me with a tale of meeting a group of Australians on the beach in Goa and them embracing him as a long lost friend with a 'tinnie' in hand, the proverbial can of beer that the Aussie is so well known for!

When at one point I asked Ronnie if people ever asked him to make them laugh when they met him in the street, his reply gave myself and the viewers a little insight into the 'real' Ronnie Corbett:

> Ronnie: Not many. The fear is that you disappoint, that you're not what they thought you would be. I think now the current crop of big comedians (I mean big stars, rather than physically big!) in America, for example, like Steve Martin and Billy Crystal, Dan Aykroyd and Chevy Chase, and John Cleese at home, tend to be more serious off than they are on. They're quite serious people and then they go into another gear to work. And I'm a bit like that…
>
> …You've (Robin) worked people in the past who are great public favourites, you know, amusing funny people and amazing funny performers. And you knew that they weren't really like that off, or all the time. I didn't know Sid very well, but Sid James was really a serious fella off…
>
> …So, people may expect me to be funny, in that case, I probably disappoint them. It's really down to you to be pleasant anyway, you know, and have a smile on your face and be nice to people, which isn't difficult.

When speaking about the people of Australia, Ronnie revealed how they viewed him and his appearance in the country:

> Ronnie: They're always very sweet and nice, but people do tend to speak as though you can't hear. You know, they say: "Goodness me, it's Ronnie Corbett," and they speak as though you're not hearing their conversation. But there always very welcoming….
>
> …Because the series *The Two Ronnies* has run in Australia for so long, and one or two other things that one has done, you know they're generally warm and pleased to see you. They're very fond of UK entertainment, they're very loyal to the UK performers.

The footage from this interview was lost for over twenty years, but I'm over the moon to say it has recently been found! It has never been seen in its entirety. Fate allowing, I hope to be able to finally show Ronnie Corbett the tape one day.

Some of the other TV appearances I made in Australia, where I was allowed to actually be myself, included a game show which, if my memory serves me right, was called the *$10,000 Pyramid.* Basically it was an Australian version of the well-known American game show. Lynn Redgrave, Dick Clark and I were the celebrities whose job it was to give the contestants their clues to the questions posed by host, Sandy Scott. Although very unsure about us at first, Sandy realised that we loved him and wanted the show to be a great success, he was fine. We all had a few silly things to say and I remember that I couldn't resist the temptation to say to sandy on camera: 'Are you wearing those socks for a bet?' Poor Sandy, he looked down with slight panic on his face only to realise that his socks were different colours! Luckily he forgave me and all was well. Scott was such a good sport and by the time we had finished our stint he understood our humour perfectly. It was a great show to be involved in.

After a tiring time playing Polonius (the chief counsellor of the King, and the father of Laertes and Ophelia) in William Shakespeare's *Hamlet*, I decided to go and visit the northern rivers, and enjoy the sun, the sea and Byron Bay. Byron Bay is a beachside town located in the far north-eastern corner of the state of New South Wales. I had just reached the grand age of fifty and decided this was the time to allow the hippie inside me to come out again. It was a time of holding radio masterclasses, putting horse and carts into Byron Bay's already over crowded streets. Horse poo and old ladies rose gardens – what more could an actor want?! It was freedom from being ruled and organised and a dream come true! Well, you could say that it was a small and amusing interlude that I wouldn't have missed for anything. Everybody who is out and about seems to end up in Byron Bay. A really exciting mix of actors, singers, writers and musicians all came to Byron.

One day I was writing while I was sitting on my veranda looking out over the Wanganui Gorge, when the phone rang. I answered and was greeted by a familiar voice I couldn't pin down.

'Hey, Robs, how the devil are you?' he asked.

After what seemed like an eternity, they finally volunteered their name before continuing.

'Thanks for the money you lent me!' he said gratefully.

Now that was well over twelve years ago and I had not heard a word from then since. I'd simply written it off as another of those things. He told me that tickets were waiting for me at Brisbane Airport and off I went to Darwin. I found myself spending a week at a property just a fraction outside the CBD. There were ten acres of stables and round yard. We then went to this incredible property way out in the middle of nowhere.

'What do you think? Half of this is yours!' my 'friend' declared.

I was shocked to say the least!

'This is what I've got together over the last few years,' he explained. 'I have a deal with Fiji to create and supply natural water to the mainland,' he said.

I knew nothing about such things and was suitably gob-smacked!

The next month was spent chasing cattle and walking along great rushing rivers trying at great lengths to avoid crocodiles that always seemed hungry.

The barbecue plate they had was big enough to handle a full grown steer or the biggest barramundi imaginable. We also lived with a forever beating sound of the huge generators that lived underground and kept the massive fridges we had at full power. It was just as well, as popping to the local shop wasn't an option – it was a hundred km away, and some roads there were difficult to navigate. The beer fridges were of the most importance as the cattle men that worked there definitely liked their beer!

One day my 'mate' and I went for miles and miles to what he said was the western boundary. That meant very little to me. Then all of a sudden on the horizon was this homestead and after staring down strong looking lean dogs on chains, that mostly looked at you with hard edged eyes and straining collars, we were greeted by this climate worn couple who pushed cold beers into our hands.

After tripping over a huge stuffed croc that just sat between a swing door onto the veranda and the living room, I settled down and listened to weather reports and market stock reports.

Later on in the day, I asked about their furniture. It was of old style dark wood, massive furniture of the Elizabethan period, maybe. What amazed me was that they had all been covered in what I imagine was sump oil, I was told that the sump oil stopped it from cracking in the unbelievable heat that was always evident in that area.

We left the farm looking at the dogs that had not changed their expressions. They looked as if they would much prefer to eat us than stare. We drove across barren land with ant hills that looked like that incredible hotel in Dubai designed to starve off the heat in the hot times and keep it in when it turned so cold that a monkey would leave home before his bits dropped off!

The next morning I was told to pack up as a monsoon was forecast. It was a case of we left immediately or we'd have been stuck there for months. Once we hit the real roads the rain started and behind us was a muddy track that soon would become impassable. With no speed limits at that time in the northern territory, the only thing to slow you down were cattle and lots of flowers pinned to rocks, trees or a post. These were a scary reminder of where an unlucky person had lost their life in an accident. Quite a few people seemed to fall asleep on the road as it was a little warmer than the roadside.

We were back in Darwin just five hours later. I left for New South Wales a few days after that, and, as promised, received a call telling me my tickets were once again at the airport. So off I went again actually rather excited about this new adventure.

Not long after I arrived back in Darwin, my chum had to go to Fiji to attend a very important meeting. A few days later there was a call for me to put cash into an offshore account. The hairs on the back of my neck began to tingle and I resisted the temptation to add more to the drain. I made some enquiries and came up against the same blocks each time. Lawyers only knew so much, accountants were even more unaware, except that a well know actor and a so-called entrepreneur had joined the team and was investing in a venture that no one really quite understood.

I left a day or so later and have heard nothing since apart from that the properties were taken back on a mortgage arrangement and my name was nowhere to be found. I cannot divulge any the names of those involved, even though I would dearly love to. But maybe, just maybe, my old 'pal' will turn up again. I must be the eternal optimist as that was fifteen years ago! I think that he's either dead or wishes that he was. I think that everyone has, at some time or another, come across people like this. The price one pays, I feel, is always cheap compared to what it could be both emotionally and financially.

My time in Australia had some very sad moments as well as some uplifting ones. There was a period when phone calls from my agent always seemed to involve requests for a eulogy for one dear friend or another. So many people in the business just started to drop like flies after a spray attack. Please don't think that I am being in any way disrespectful. It's just that from Steve Marriot to Yootha Joyce, and Diana Coupland to Tony Jackson, the list seemed to go on and on. There were times when one thought how long before it's my name up there?

I get so confused by the people who say they know what death all about, because I really don't. All I know is I am not going to see that person again, and why not?

So there's no closure. I know many people in the industry who have passed away, and they all had so much still to offer. I guess that we're born, we're there and then we're not. It's a never ending circle that some of us never really learn to comprehend.

This brings me on to when I was hosting *Opportunity Knocks* back in New Zealand, we used to record the show at the Civic Theatre in Christchurch. There was a phone backstage, but if a call came through it was usually answered in the OB van. This was the van that connected the theatre to the nearby studio. On one particular evening they missed it and one of our stage hands answered it. We were in the very last commercial break before the end of the show for that week. The guy who answered the phone called me over.

'Robin, it's for you mate!' he said cheerily.

My immediate thought was that it must be Tom my producer in the OB van with a private message that he didn't want to share through the floor manager. I took the phone.

'Yes, Robin here,' I replied.

I was the greeted by a man with an Indian accent who asked me if I was Robin Steuer, known also as Robin Stewart. Thinking it was a joke, I decided to go along with it.

'Yes, tis I!' I said in a carefree fashion.

'I am calling from London, England, to inform you that your father Maxamilian Steuer died an hour ago,' he informed me.

He then gave me the name of the hospital.

'This can't be right, he's in France,' I told him.

'No, Mr. Steuer, he IS here,' he replied. Well, he is here, but he's dead. This is the hospital. I suggest if you have any enquiries you phone back tomorrow and ask to speak to the relevant department.'

And that was that.

What I didn't know at that point was my producer had picked up the phone in the OB van and listened in to the call. He then rearranged the last segment of the show so that a female singer was moved from first act of the last segment to the last act so she closed the show. The song that she was set to perform was 'Memories', and the producer asked the director to make sure that he caught the tear that would be in my eye so that it could be super-imposed over the singer's face and make great TV. I didn't find out until later, so I never had a chance to question this decision.

It's a funny thing how fate sometimes brings people into your orbit. Just after my wife, Bertie, had first joined me in Australia, I got a call from a journalist and writer who lives not far away from my Australian base. Her name is Candida Baker, and it turned out that she's also a mad-keen horse person. Candida was introduced to me by my old friend Chris O'Reilly and she wanted to write a magazine profile on me for *Good Weekend*, the Saturday magazine for the *Sydney Morning Herald*. Candida takes up the story:

> Candida: I know what you're thinking…,' said Robin, giving me an actor's smile – a twinkling, flashing smile, a naughty smile. 'You're thinking, Christ, here goes another Luvvie, droning on about himself, drinking and carrying on, aren't you?' Oops. Caught out. 'It's written all over your face,' he continued. 'Actor's daughter. Bored witless by actors. And who wouldn't be? I'm bored of them myself – bored of myself too, come to think of it.' He roared with laughter. The problem when Robin laughs is that it brings on a coughing attack. The emphysema that has claimed seventy-five percent of

his lung capacity making its sudden deathly presence felt. As the fit passes, he smiles again – a genuine, I'm still here sort of smile which is infectious in its optimism.

We were sitting in the restaurant of the Bangalow Hotel, brought together by a long-time friend of Robin's, a Kyogle farmer, Chris O'Reilly. There was Stewart, O'Reilly, myself, and Stewart's soon-to-be wife, Bertie, which in itself is as sweet a love story as you could ever read about. O'Reilly thought it was time that Robin talked about his life – about his career as a child star, his years spent playing Sid James' son in *Bless this House*, about his carousing and drinking days – how he ended up running an equestrian centre in the Darling Downs, breeding and competing Arab endurance horses.

Of course, it then turns out that Robin was a friend of my father, the late George Baker, the very chivalrous actor in so many films. They not only shared the delights of big cars – i.e. the Rolls Royce a big favourite with both of them – and a love of horses and indoor games such as poker. They only ever shared a stage together and that was to host the Feltex Awards in New Zealand and give out the much-prized award for most popular TV celebrity in the country. It was a top night unfortunately they did not manage to get to the races as George had to get back to England post haste, and Robin was filming *Opportunity Knocks*. Both Robin and my father were rebels in their own right and in their own way. There are times when Robin reminds me of him because of his attitude towards life.

I was sorry to learn that George had died the previous year. We also found out that Candida had spent a large part of her misspent youth hanging out at all my old Soho haunts, and behaving almost as badly as me. This was before she decided to become the really boring person she is today! But we formed a great friendship, and Candida and Bertie immediately ganged up on me – as women do – and had a fine time picking over my many faults. She and her partner Greg came to our wedding, and Candida was our wedding photographer.

It became a bit of a routine to drop into Candida's place and have a cuppa or a meal, and chat about the old days while she helped me update my website. I have a love of words – as she does too – but she likes them spelt correctly and in the right order, which is handy for me!

As Candida mentioned, George and I only worked together once, and that was to present the Feltex awards as special guests in New Zealand, where he'd been filming the *Ngaio Marsh* detective series. Our paths had obviously crossed before but on that occasion we found out that we had a lot in common. I think we were partners in crime when it came to the joys of living, and Candida after only a minimal acquaintance with me, wasn't surprised that we'd got on so well – even though on that occasion we actually didn't get pissed. Unusual for both of us!

Another tale I must share with you about my Australia days is about an incredible entertainer called Ricky May. Ricky was a Maori who I had the honour of presenting an award to in the late Seventies. He was not only one of New Zealand's favourite sons, but was an integral part of the Australian music scene. As well as being a vocalist, he played drums and piano and was also known as a variety entertainer until his untimely death in 1988. I will never forget when I was involved in stopping the open cut mine going into Yarramalong

Valley, Ricky and his wife turned up at the farm in the early hours of the morning with his musical director, Jamie Rigg, and an enormous bowl of salad! Ricky ate and sang and then played a charity football game at an event that we organised in the valley for all the local kids. Memorably, he did the Haka with over twenty children in front of the goal posts in order to stop the opposing team from scoring. All this having driven over two hundred km from Wollongong, where he was performing the night before. Ricky was a great and well-respected entertainer who did so much for charity. Is it any wonder that he's so missed by all those of us who loved him?

We all have a bucket list of dreams, I achieved many of mine. But I wish I'd had the opportunity to travel the great open doors in a gypsy caravan. Yes, I know, who wants to travel miles with the sight of a horse's behind in your face? Well, me! I would have loved the tranquillity and being at one with nature. I know the idea might sound strange to some, but I would have found it a joyful experience. Sadly, the nearest I ever got to owning a gypsy caravan was when my character Mike Abbott, and his sister Sally, bought one in an episode of *Bless this House*!

I have always marvelled at the lack of interest that wildlife takes of a human when he or she is aboard a horse. The animal accepts totally that the horse is of no threat whatsoever, and one can watch foxes at play, or any number of marsupials, without any fear being given off by the horse's presence. And that's when you get to see and feel so many different aspects of nature – and all while benefitting from incredible amazing views! It's certainly a luxury that has to be experienced to be appreciated and believed. I consider myself so have been very lucky that I was privy to such memorable moments. Each is deeply engraved within my memory and helped to make all the many unhappy moments pale into insignificance.

Endurance riders' motto is 'To complete is to win'. For those of you who don't know, endurance riders are the purists, the adventurers and the riders who make a living out of selling on their competitive horses, mainly Arabians. They buy horses world-wide and have created an amazingly competitive market place. I have bred and sold horses into this market and have seen what the money side of the sport can create in people.

One early morning, I was driving down the hill leading to Bonalbo in northern New South Wales and looking down on the show grounds. I suddenly had this vision of the whole place full of horse rigs and smoking open fires and lots and lots of horses. And that was it, the Bonalbo Bash was born – well inside my head anyway! I thought it would make an appealing attraction. The old Australian show grounds are the most incredible open spaces in most country towns with buildings that relate back to yesteryear when every farmer weather stock or produce would, at some time or other, be at the showground showing their livestock or produce. It was, apart from the hotel, a major part of every country town, no matter how large or small. Its communities were always maintaining the buildings to keep everything up to scratch. Bearing this in mind, I thought what a great idea to have an endurance ride at our own showground.

Having managed to get my idea passed by the committee, the hard work started in earnest. A course had to be laid out, which meant contacting every farmer in the district to see if permission could be obtained to use parts of their properties. This sounds simple, but it was far from easy to persuade a farmer to agree to have people traversing across their beloved pastures and hills and dales. Stock had to be moved to accommodate the tracks that would be used, and markers had to be placed at relevant intervals so that riders don't get lost. I was only putting on a forty km novice ride and an eighty km open ride over, I might add, pretty rugged terrain. Arrows in different colours had to be obtained and then attached to trees or fences, and anything that was readably visible to a rider travelling at speeds of up to, and on some occasions, over twenty-five to thirty km per hour.

My first, and most radical mistake, was that I got the local school to help make the arrows. My choice of colours was my second mistake. I chose green and so the first leg was now marked with green arrows. What a fool! Trees have green leaves, and my arrows blended in famously. The complaint box was brimming over! Having overcome this unforgivable mistake, and appeased the upset front runners who wanted fast times to go in their horses' log book for its resale, the day progressed.

I had arranged that the vets would be at the show grounds until nearly four am on the Saturday morning. That way people could leave work Friday night, and travel through the night. Some of them drove hundreds of km to compete. Usually they would travel to such an event on a Saturday, have their horses inspected by the vet, start the ride in the dark on the Sunday morning, and get it all over and done with by late afternoon. Then they would take their horses to be inspected by the vet again, attend the awards presentation, pack up and drive the many miles home totally exhausted! I thought that if everybody came on the Friday night, or early on the Saturday morning, they could ride out on their relevant first leg of their designated ride in the early morning light, and the front runners in the open ride, being eighty km, would be finished in four hours, and the tail enders would be completely finished by five thirty pm. They could then have their horse inspected by the vet again, settle their horses for the night, shower in time for dinner, and then party for as long as they liked. The presentation would be held at about nine thirty on the Sunday morning. This would give everybody time to travel home at a leisurely pace throughout the Sunday. Thankfully, all my plans came to fruition and it worked! We had three bands playing through the night, an unbelievable roast dinner and a Saturday market running all day to keep the spectators amused while the horses were on track. I was forgiven the green arrow mistake and the best party ride was born!

I kept the Bonalbo Bash going for five years and was blessed with amazing sponsors. It became known as a very hard ride with great food and the best party atmosphere! As the years went on, I added film screenings which ran throughout the night, with people spread out around raging fires, and bands playing in another area of the showground. It was so much fun and a great weekend. Unfortunately, I had to stop staging the annual event when my health started to go downhill. The event is sadly missed, but never forgotten. Even now you can go to a ride and see people wearing their best conditioned jackets with the Bonalbo Bash emblazoned across the back. I always have a deep feeling of pride whenever I see someone wearing one. I believe the parties we had are still often talked about around the camp fires at night!

From the age of sixteen I have had a love affair with the dreaded nicotine. I took to cigarette smoking like a duck takes to water, with a flurry of wings and a great inhalation. Let's face it, all men wanted to be the

Marlborough man back then. Well, I certainly did, and from the blonde tobacco to the French black, I smoked like a demon possessed. When I pulled on a cigarette I took the smoke in all the way down to my toes and back again. Then I used to let it filter back up into my nose after it gently filtered out of my mouth on its way back.

Not until I was sixty did I start to think that anything was wrong with my health. Then I started to feel a bit short of breath. Stupidly, I ignored the hint that all was not well – that was until the day I collapsed in the stallion paddock and ended up in intensive care with pneumonia. I was then diagnosed with chronic emphysema. This was such a shock as I really did think that all that was wrong was that I was a bit short of breath. No such luck, my lungs were rebelling after years of abuse.

The aftermath of the intensive care, and subsequent tests over the following year, was devastating. At one stage, my lungs gave up and my throat closed. My friends all thought I was going to die. The looks on their faces were awful. My whole way of life changed literally overnight. I could no longer ride my beloved horses or carry their feed out to them each day. It went from being sheer joy to one of the hardest jobs I had ever done. Caressing the proud necks and rippling muscles of the horses turned into hours of agony. I felt a real hopelessness. I had already done the recluse stage of my life. I was still appearing on game shows and being very careful not to exert myself. It was woeful. I used the excuse that I was writing more than before. Although this was true, and I love writing, it was not by choice during this period of my life.

The fact that I could no longer ride my horses was a killer. My last ride was at a place called Imbil. It's a pretty hard track, but all my horses enjoyed it, and so did I. I found out on that fateful day I came in just behind the winners who had completed the eighty km ride in just under four hours. The only problem was as they rode towards me and, then into the night thinking that I was finishing fast, I had only just finished the first forty km and was the very last person on the track. I slide off my faithful boomer, an Arabian who had such amazing attitude and always gave his all. A friend of mine then took him out to the vetting and my farm manager helped me back to the truck, where I collapsed. We obviously had to retire due to rider illness.

It was long before I went through the traumatic experience of being told by doctors at my hospital bedside that it was basically all over for me. And so because I believed that I was going to the big TV studio in the sky, I cancelled my private health cover and decided to invest my money in bottles of red wine instead. Well, if one is going to go, enjoy the red wine, that's what I say! Then, out of nowhere, a specialist came to me and said: 'Robin, I can fix you'. I couldn't believe it. Before long I was undergoing revolutionary valve treatment. They put two valves into my right lung and told me that I was all fixed! I was over the moon! A bit of rehabilitation and life will have a bit of the old buzz about it again, I thought. I went and did a pilot for a new show that I had up my sleeve and felt positive about life again.

I flew back to England to be with my family, and then life fell apart again when I discovered that the valves were in the wrong place. I continually pray that once my lungs are suitably plugged up, I will at least be able to ride again, if not at great speed or with the same gusto. We will see how that all goes as the time grows closer to the valves being moved. Should the operation take place, then the surgeon will be one Mr. Shah. Shah is an expert in the field of respiratory lung reduction procedures involving pulmonary valves. He's the leading authority in this field, and is based at the Brompton Hospital in the UK. I hope Mr. Shah's expertise will allow me to live to fight many, many more days on this planet.

I shamefully admit that smoking was something I used to love to do. It might shock you to learn that I would probably have still smoked even if I had known then what I know now. Unfortunately, the ramifications are drastic and truly radical. I watched Sid James as he stopped smoking everything until even his trusty pipe was no longer in use. If only I had taken more notice of him, then the dreaded emphysema may not have got me.

I look at life now through totally different eyes. Every breath is just so precious now, and every morning is a blessing. I will beat this and hope to do the things that I love again. It will be a hard road, but I will get there. I just hope that if one person can look at what I have written about smoking, then revealing my health problems will have all been worthwhile.

There are always many doors that close during one's life. I know that there were so many opportunities that I probably missed by bad judgment. But then life, by its very nature, always has its ups and downs. And most, if not all of them, are valid in their own way. I think that we all mess up our private lives at some point or other. I just hope that I have been forgiven by the people involved for all of the indiscretions I made.

I think that I personally have enjoyed life far too much. As a result, I have paid the price quite heavily. For example, during the course of writing this book I suffered my second stroke in twelve years. This recent one was a bit of a shock to the system. I thought that I had my stress problem under control just by laughing as much as possible. I must admit that as I haven't smoked since 2006, so I was a little angry with my body for letting me down. But the damage has been done, hence the stroke, I guess. The good thing is that it wasn't a major stroke, and the tests suggest that if a little more blood can get through to my brain, then all will be well. I've been ordered to follow a whole new diet which means I now have to eat a number of things I don't really like. But for the sake of spending more time on this planet, it will all be worth it.

Call it a sixth sense, or whatever you will, but I have often had premonitions about things going wrong or potentially going wrong. The following email (edited slightly inclusion within this book) which I received from a taxi driver forty years after we met, is arguably proof of this:

Dear Robin,

Do you remember many years ago when you were in the TV show *Bless this House*, and you lived in Camden near the Brecknock? And do you remember taking a taxi home, and when getting out of the taxi on the corner of Torriano Avenue, asking the driver to make you a promise that every time the driver used crossroads on the Camden Road to take the utmost care? Do you recall how adamant you were that the driver made a promise to you to take every precaution when crossing the Camden Road from Camden Park Road into Torriano Avenue? You were so concerned, that you made me promise that I would do as you asked. To be honest, I never thought about it that often. That was until one night in the early hours of the morning in heavy rain some ten years later. I was making that crossing on a green light when your face appeared in my mind's eye. In fact, it seemed to spread across my windscreen. I braked as hard as I could, screeching to a halt on a green light. My passenger ended up on the floor, so he never saw the car scream through a red light at high speed coming from the Holloway direction – a blind spot for me – which probably would have killed us both.

So whatever prompted you that evening to ask that of me most certainly saved me and my passenger from a possible fatal accident. I would like to thank you most sincerely whether you remember it or not. If you ever find yourself back in England, I'll buy you a drink!

Michael Pollington

I guess many of us have had these experiences. It's just that quite often we're not aware of just how poignant they are, or could be, at the time. I must admit that sometimes I've often felt a fool when trying to explain these sudden overriding feelings.

I don't know what inspired me to warn Michael that night. Was it a premonition? Or was it just common sense? Either way, receiving this email forty years after the event was, in some ways, quite scary but reassuring. But I remember how important it felt at the time to let this cab driver know how terribly dangerous that particular crossing was. Well, Michael, I am back in the UK now and I would love that beer! I'm so pleased that you were both safe.

I was delighted when I was asked to appear at Memorabilia, Britain's biggest collectors' event, at the NEC in Birmingham, during a weekend in late

November 2013. This was the first time I had ever appeared at a convention of this type, and Bertie and I didn't know exactly what to expect. But so many people came up to say thank you for the enjoyment that my appearances on film and TV had brought them, that we were both left feeling quite overwhelmed. The *Bless this House* fans were particularly enthusiastic. It appears that the whole Abbott family have been a big part of their lives. I know it's a weekend I know I will never forget!

Following another spell in hospital just before Christmas 2013, Bertie and I made our way to Central Hall Westminster, London, on Saturday 25th January 2014. The reaction I received from the fans who attended was equally as enthusiastic! What was quite touching was that many of those who I met said they had travelled all the way down to London to the event from up north. And for the first time ever at a public event, the *Bless this House* fans had the extra bonus of meeting Mike Abbot and Sally Abbott together – yes, Sally Geeson, was also there!

Sally and I were reunited again on Saturday 1 March 2014 when we appeared together at Kaleidoscope's Thames TV event in Stourbridge in the West Midlands. I was amazed at the number of people who attended. The age range varied from seven year-old children all the way up to senior citizens. Sally and I both did a thirty minute interview each in front of an audience. Working with Sally again was, in the words of Mike Abbott, a real blast! I am pleased to say there are now plans for Sally and I to attend a number of events together in the future, including those being organised by the Heritage Foundation.

In the spring of 2014, I attended a luncheon organised by the Heritage Foundation which was held in honour of my old *Bless this House* mate, Lionel Blair. It was wonderful to see so many of Lionel's showbiz colleagues paying tribute to him. I love attending such events as they gives me the opportunity to meet up with lots of people in showbiz I haven't seen in years!

Recently I started to wonder what would have become of Mike Abbott and Sally Abbott in *Bless this House* – if they'd been real people! I personally think that Sally would have left home, got married and had a couple of kids. As for Mike? Well, I think he would probably be living in a teepee at the bottom of Sally's garden! I am convinced he would have gone on to become a sort of Peter Pan character and refused to grow up. He'd probably still have his causes, and be a rebel in his own way. I always thought he was like a little pirate without a ship. He had sails, but no ship. To him he was successful, he lived in a dream and was very much his own person.

As for me and the future? To be honest, I am still learning how to cope with the various challenges that my ongoing health problems have presented. But ironically these problems have given me a whole new way of looking at life. I believe we take too much for granted – some of us more than others. The best lesson I've learned during my years on this planet is that we're all responsible for our own downfalls, including me. The simple answer is that we need to learn from our mistakes – and not repeat them!

Despite all my many ups and downs, I personally think I have been very lucky. I now live happily with my wife, Bertie, in Dorset, with happy memories of our lovely 2012 wedding in Coffs Harbour back in Australia, still very fresh in my mind. I have been blessed with four grandchildren so far, and I hope all of them will, when the time is right, read this book by their grandfather.

Now, as you reach the end of this little book, I would like to leave you with this thought:

> Today has been pure magic, and all our tomorrows will be even better.

Until we meet again…

Robin

Afterword

I feel very privileged to have been asked to write an afterword for Robin's book. I have read with great interest about his life, work and family.

I am very lucky to have very fond memories of the Bless this House days. A young teenager at the time, I enjoyed going to the recordings and was in awe of Robin and Sally – my on screen siblings! The public's affection for the Abbott family was reflected in the extraordinary ratings and enormous popularity of the series. The funny and clever writers hit the mark exactly, and with the hugely talented William G. leading the team, Dad's wonderful and intuitive understanding of performance, a unique chemistry between him, Diana, Robin and Sally: no wonder viewers wanted to watch!

The James family thank you Robin for writing about those happy times.

A special memory and legacy for us all to be able to share.

Susan James
August 2014

Robin Stewart
Credits

This section features just a small selection of Robin's many theatre, film and TV credits:

Theatre

The Complaisant Love (1959)

Will You Walk a Little Faster (1960)

Camelot (1960)

Billy Bunter Meets Magic

The Man Most Likely To (1972)

Two and Two Make Sex (1975)

The Murder Game (1976)

Up 'n' Under (1986)

Hamlet (1996)

Film

Greyfriars Bobby (1961)

Vice Versa (1961)

H.M.S. Defiant (1962)

Masters of Venus (1962)

1. **Sabotage**
2. **Lost In Space**
3. **The Men With Six Fingers**
4. **The Thing In The Crater**
5. **Prisoners Of Venus**
6. **The Killer Virus**
7. **Kill On Sight**
8. **Attack**

Tamahine (1963)

Be My Guest (1965)

The Haunted House of Horror (1969)

Cromwell (1970)

The Legend of the 7 Golden Vampires (1974)

Adventures of a Private Eye (1977)

Pacific Banana (1981)

Casino Reef (1998)

TV

Deadline Midnight (1960)

24 Hours in a Woman's Life

Dixon of Dock Green (1968)

Softly Softly (1969)

Bless this House (1971-1976)

Series One

1. **The Generation Gap**
2. **Mum's The Word**
3. **Father's Day**
4. **Be It Ever So Humble**
5. **5. Another Fine Mess**
6. **For Whom The Bells Toll**
7. **A Woman's Place**
8. **The Day Of Rest**
9. **Make Love, Not War**
10. **Charity Begins At Home**
11. **If The Dog Collar Fits... Wear It!**
12. **The Morning After The Night Before**

Series Two

1. **Two Heads Are Better Than One**
2. **Love Me, Love My Tree**
3. **It's All In The Mind**
4. **Another Lost Weekend**
5. **Parents Should Be Seen And Not Heard**
6. **Strangers In The Night**
7. **Get Me To The Match On Time**
8. **Wives And Lovers**
9. **Never Again On Sunday**
10. **People In Glass Houses**
11. **A Rolls By Any Other Name**
12. **A Touch Of The Unknown**

Series Three

1. **It Comes To Us All In The End**

2. Tea For Two And Four For Tea
3. To Tell Or Not To Tell
4. Blood Is Thicker Than Water
5. One Good Turn Deserves A Bother
6. The Loneliness Of The Short Distance Walker
7. Watch The Birdie
8. Will The Real Sid Abbott Please Stand Up
9. Atishoo! Atishoo! We All Fall Down
10. Entente Not So Cordiale
11. I'm Not jealous, I'll Kill Him
12. A Girl's Worst Friend Is Her Father

Series Four

1. Money Is The Root Of...
2. And They Will Come Home
3. Who's Minding The Baby?
4. A Beef In His Bonnet
5. The Bells Are Ringing
6. The First 25 Years Are The Worst

Series Five

1. They Don't Write Songs Like That Anymore
2. The Gipsy's Warning
3. The Biggest Woodworm In The World
4. Home Tweet Home
5. You're Never Too Old To Be Young
6. The Policeman, The Paint And The Pirates
7. Happy Birthday Sid
8. Freedom Is…
9. Mr. Chairman...
10. And Afterwards At...

Series Six

1. **The Frozen Limit**
2. **Beautiful Dreamer**
3. **Fish With Everything**
4. **The Naked Paperhanger**
5. **Remember Me?**
6. **Something Of Value**
7. **Men Of Consequence**
8. **Skin Deep**
9. **Friends And Neighbours**
10. **Well, Well, Well**
11. **The Phantom Pools Winner**
12. **A Matter Of Principle**
13. **Some Enchanted Evening**

Rembrandt (1971)

The Troubleshooters (1972)

Whodunnit? (1975)

Opportunity Knocks (1977)

Celebrity Squares (1977)

Leap in the Dark (1977)

The Timeless Land (1980)

The Young Doctors (1981)

Hopgood (1981)

Punishment (1981)

A Christmas Carol (1982)

Great Expectations (1982)

David Copperfield (1983)

Sherlock Holmes and the Valley of Fear (1983)

Sherlock Holmes and the Sign of Four (1983)

Sherlock Holmes and the Baskerville Curse (1983)

Sweet and Sour (1984)

Five Mile Creek (1984)

A Tale of Two Cities (1984)

Sons and Daughters (1984 -1985)

Runaway Island: The Treasure of the Conquistadors

Nicholas Nickleby (TV Film, 1985)

Midweek Live (1990)

Welcher & Welcher (2003)

Lightning Source UK Ltd.
Milton Keynes UK
UKOW03f1505290914

239375UK00001B/5/P